WORSHIP WITHOUT WORDS

THE SIGNS AND SYMBOLS *of* OUR FAITH

EXPANDED EDITION

Patricia S. Klein

PARACLETE PRESS

BREWSTER, MASSACHUSETTS

Worship Without Words, Expanded Edition

2007 First Printing Expanded Edition

Copyright © 2000, 2007 by Patricia S. Klein

ISBN 13: 978-1-55725-504-4

Unless otherwise designated, Scripture quotations are taken from the Holy Bible, New International Version®. NIV®. ©1973, 1978 by International Bible Society. Used by permission of Zondervan Publishing House. All rights reserved.

Special acknowledgment to C.R. Gibson, the publisher of *A Dictionary of Church Terms and Symbols*, which formed the foundation for this book.

Illustrations on cover and in text used by permission of The C.R. Gibson Company. © 1974 by The C.R. Gibson Company.

Quoted portions of Latin liturgy and their English translations are from *St. John's Missal for Every Day*, published by Brepols' Catholic Press, New York, NY, 1950.

Original illustrations in text provided by the artists of The Community of Jesus, Inc.

Library of Congress Cataloging-in-Publication Data
Klein, Patricia.
    Worship without words : the signs and symbols of our faith / Patricia S. Klein.
    — Expanded ed.
        p. cm.
    Includes bibliographical references and index.
    ISBN 978-1-55725-504-4 (pbk.)
    1. Christian art and symbolism. I. Title.
    BV150.K54 2007
    246-dc21   2006033076

10 9 8 7 6 5 4 3 2 1

Published by Paraclete Press
Brewster, Massachusetts
www.paracletepress.com
Printed in the United States of America

To Joanne,
who understood more than most
the power of images and words,
and whose faith was always filled
with wonder and laughter.
You are missed.

Contents

Introduction to the Second Edition

Generally, I don't enjoy revisiting work. I'm the sort of person who likes to do a task once and move on to another. That's why chores are such a challenge to me. Laundering and folding the same towel again and again seems to me to be, well, a chore. I'm better with errands, but only just. I long ago determined that, for me, anything that is not a chore or an errand is by definition fun.

Revisiting this book has been neither a chore nor an errand. It has been fun. Fun not because the actual research and writing has been fun, although there have been moments. No, expanding this book has been fun because it's turned into an opportunity to remember, much like reading old letters or looking at old vacation snapshots. Remembering is both a great joy and a profound gift.

In recent years, to my great frustration, words and names more often escape me, and I forget commitments or misplace bills or keys with annoying regularity. As I struggle to make my synapses connect and keep my dignity intact, I am reminded that without our memories we are simply shells, bodies without content, books without words.

Experts tell us that like so many other things in life, remembering well requires practice: The more you remember, the better you remember. This is a spiritual truth as well. In Scripture, one of God's most frequent commands is "Remember." Remember, you were slaves in Egypt and the Lord your God redeemed you. Celebrate Passover so that you remember that I am one who delivered you. Remember my covenant. When you eat this bread and drink this cup, remember me.

Worship is wholly dependent on the truth that the more we remember, the better we remember. When we encounter a particular piece of architecture or a vestment, a sacrament or a piece of art, we engage both the present and the past. All of our senses—hearing, seeing, touching, smelling, tasting—engage the present, while our souls remember the great meanings, the stories, the experiences that recall those occasions when God reached out to meet us, both individually and in community.

And the beauty of symbols is that they provide us with a sort of shorthand for remembering, simple things that tell great stories. When we see a manger, what we see is an animal's feeding trough; what we remember is a great story filled with angels and miracles and wonder—God's intersection with humanity. When we see a drawing of a whale, we remember the recalcitrant Jonah. When we see a shepherd carrying a lamb, we remember Jesus and his care for us.

In this edition I explore a bit more of the symbolism found in the Western Christian art tradition, especially Medieval and Renaissance art. New here are symbols found in some of the more traditional themes of the Church, such as Old Testament saints, the Virgin Mary, the lives of saints, as well as more dramatic themes such as Sin and Temptation and Last Things. There are great volumes that offer considerably more detail than can be presented in a small handbook like this, but I've tried to include the more common symbols and images, especially those associated with biblical narratives and language.

God wants us to remember him. Signs and symbols are curious and interesting and perhaps even entertaining in an odd sort of way. But they are finally about remembering God: his Word, his promises, his intentions, his love, his greatness and glory. Remembering God is an act of worship; signs and symbols are merely a gate.

Welcome!

Patricia S. Klein
PENTECOST 2006

Introduction to the First Edition

Many years ago, on an uptown pilgrimage to the Cloisters in New York City, I found myself immersed in an entire language of faith that was completely foreign to my own Christian experience. The Cloisters (part of the Metropolitan Museum of Art) was created from the ruins of several European monasteries and forms an ensemble of rooms and gardens that feature a treasury of medieval exhibits. Visitors are transported into eleventh-century Europe, where Christian faith was modeled in the monastic community.

In the Middle Ages, I discovered, Christianity was visual. Architecture, windows, ornaments, tapestries, paintings, tombs—no matter where I looked, I saw faith represented not by words, but by images. I knew instinctively that all these images carried stories, but I might as well have been dropped into Pakistan for all that I could understand what many of those stories were. And sadly I must confess that this Midwestern Protestant was more than a little uncomfortable. For the first time in my life I encountered the reliquary and the triptych (not to be confused with AAA's TripTik®). I could touch and see the symbols of faith in stone and fabric and metal.

Then I discovered the tapestry of the Apostles' Creed. Filling up most of the wall in one of the corridors, there hung a beautiful tapestry in which the entirety of the Creed was woven in symbols. I studied each symbol and haltingly recited the words of the Creed, imprinting on my soul a visual memory of the ancient words that I had only recently begun to include in my weekly worship.

In this remarkable weaving, my personal Rosetta stone, I began a new journey into a worship experience that was not dependent upon words. My faith from childhood had always been rooted in words, specifically the Word of God or the Bible. In my fundamentalist world, symbolism was confined to the Sunday school song "The

Wordless Book" or the simple cross that hung at the front of the church. But now, I discovered the most ancient vocabulary of worship.

The history of Christian worship is bathed in symbolism, beginning with the symbols from the Jewish Scriptures: the rainbow God gave Noah, the bronze serpent that Moses raised to bring healing, and the Passover meal established as a memorial to God's rescue of the Israelites from Egypt. Jesus himself understood the importance of symbols in his own worship and in his teaching: "Just as Moses lifted up the serpent in the wilderness…"; "I am the bread of life"; "I am the light of the world"; "I am the door"; "I am the good shepherd"; "I am the true vine"; and of course, his final meal with his disciples which he established as a memorial for those who love him.

Our worship is filled with signs and symbols. "When you do this, remember this." We are physical creatures, and our physical nature and world are God's gift to us. God uses physical things to communicate the transcendent, knowable things to communicate the unknowable. Our symbols of faith and worship remind; they teach; they translate God into our everyday experience. Indeed, these are sacraments, which according to The Book of Common Prayer, "are outward and visible signs of inward and spiritual grace."

In order to understand the symbolism in our worship and liturgy, first imagine a world with limited access to the basic necessities of life. Living with limitations is difficult to imagine in a culture where we have access upon demand to almost everything we want, but in days past, basic limitations defined not only people's everyday lives but also their faith and worship.

These limitations were largely tied to the availability of natural resources. Light was limited, in general, to daylight. Water was limited and so, therefore, was cleanliness. Bread was limited in large part to what could be created in the home. Social mobility was limited—for the most part, one's birth defined one's life.

But most significantly of all for worship, literacy was limited. Most cultures in the ancient world did not place a high value on literacy, with the Jews being the most obvious exception to this generality. As the child of Judaism, Christianity would also come to place great value on reading and writing. In general, however, people could not read. Christian worship was not an exercise in reading; it was an exercise in hearing and watching. Later, when Christianity had spread from Rome throughout Europe, converting people of many languages and cultures, worship was conducted in Latin, limiting worship literacy once again to those who could understand Latin. It was in this environment that colors and gestures and symbols became the language of worship. One did not need to read in order to understand what was happening in the Mass. It became possible to worship without words.

Everything in worship has its roots deep in history, and most of the liturgical traditions of the Western Church are anchored in the church of ancient Rome. The model of liturgical churches is not democracy, but monarchy. To the modern mind, formed by democratic values, monarchy is a foreign and perhaps unsavory concept. But the self-described purpose of Jesus' ministry was to create a kingdom, and the monarchy was the dominant model of human government when the Church was born. Without doubt, there are echoes of royalty in many of the features of liturgical worship. And if monarchy defined the appearance of the Church, monasticism defined the substance of worship, setting forth the disciplines, the values, the practices of daily worship and life in Christ. Monarchy and monasticism together characterize most aspects of liturgical life today.

Understanding the liturgical church requires understanding a few fundamentals. This is particularly true for Protestants whose worship practices were thoroughly bathed in the Reformation, moving away from liturgical worship.

First and foremost, God is present, in all his holiness and "other-ness," at the altar in the elements of the Eucharist. The altar is the center of liturgical worship and is the sign of the presence of God in the Holy Eucharist. While churches may differ theologically regarding the substance of the bread and wine, all acknowledge the

Eucharist as the central memorial of Christ's sacrifice for us, and the altar as the table from which this memorial is celebrated. What may seem at first blush to be exaggerated and perhaps a tad idolatrous (especially to the low-church Protestant) becomes the natural and necessary response to the Presence of God. The altar is not simply furniture; the sanctuary is not merely space. God is present at the altar, and his Presence fills the sanctuary, just as he was present in the Holy of Holies. The Presence of God in the Eucharist and at the altar is the key to understanding many other aspects of liturgical worship and practice. The second distinction of liturgical churches is that baptism is the defining moment of faith, signifying the beginning of one's membership in the Body of Christ. In many nonliturgical churches more importance is placed on the profession of faith, "accepting Christ as personal Savior," and baptism is the public act subsequent to that profession.

The purpose of this book is not simply to define the various aspects of liturgical Christianity, while that is certainly what I intend it to do. My hope is that by learning and understanding the various parts of this tradition, we can disarm our objections and fears and learn to participate in the worship. In order to worship, we need to forget ourselves, to lose ourselves in the Presence of God, which is impossible if we resist participating by asking questions and objecting to certain practices. Then our attention is focused not on God, but on our anxieties and objections. In addition, if we are unfamiliar with liturgical practices, we can be self-conscious, another impediment to authentic worship.

You may worship in a "low church" which is less ceremonial and formal than a "high church," whose worship overflows with "smells and bells." Or you may decide that the formality and ceremony of the high church enhances your worship experience. Either way, each of us typically is concerned that we are "liturgically cool." No one wants to stand or kneel at the wrong time, and everyone wants to know how to receive Communion properly. Basically, we want to understand the unspoken language of worship however it is celebrated. One good rule is: "Don't assume everyone else knows what is going on." The truth is that, in general, there are the rules, and then there's what's done. One can learn much about participating in a particular worship service simply by watching other worshipers. But if certain practices are uncomfortable, then concentrate on worship, and perhaps later these practices will become part of your own worship.

The Church is vital and dynamic, as are our lives in Christ. May our vibrant worship of God, our celebration of Christ's death and resurrection, and our empowerment by the Holy Spirit lead and enable us as we grow in our faith.

> *Open the eyes of our hearts to know you, who alone are highest amid the highest, and ever abide holy amid the holy. You bring down the haughtiness of the proud, and scatter the devices of the people. You set up the lowly on high, and the lofty you cast down. Riches and poverty, death and life, are in your hand; you alone are the discerner of every spirit, and the God of all flesh. Your eyes behold the depths and survey the works of humankind; you are the aid of those in peril, the savior of them that despair, the creator and overseer of everything that has breath. . . . Deliver the afflicted, pity the lowly, raise the fallen, reveal yourself to the needy, heal the sick, and bring home your wandering people. Feed the hungry, ransom the captive, support the weak, comfort the fainthearted. Let all the nations of the earth know that you are God alone, that Jesus Christ is your child, and that we are your people and the sheep of your pasture. (Clement)[1]*

Patricia S. Klein
PENTECOST 2000

Note: Terms that appear in *italic* are alternative terms for the main entry. Terms that appear in **semi-bold** have their own entries elsewhere in the book. Please refer to the index for specific locations.

WORSHIP WITHOUT WORDS

ONE
Sacred Places, Sacred Spaces

When you step through the doorway of a church you are leaving the outer world behind and entering an inner world. The outside world is a fair place abounding in life and activity, but also a place with a mingling of the base and ugly. It is a sort of marketplace, crossed and recrossed by all and sundry. Perhaps "unholy" is not quite the word for it, yet there is something profane about the world. Behind the church doors is an inner place, separated from the market place, a silent, consecrated and holy spot. It is very certain that the whole world is the work of God and His gift to us, that we may meet Him anywhere, that everything we receive is from God's hand, and, when received religiously, is holy. Nevertheless men have always felt that certain precincts were in a special manner set apart and dedicated to God. (Romano Guardini)[2]

ECCLESIASTICAL BUILDINGS

Ecclesiastical buildings are divided into two classes: churches and oratories.

church. A house of God, dedicated exclusively for public worship. A sacred building dedicated to divine worship for the use of all the faithful and the public exercise of religion. There are five kinds of churches:

- **basilica**. A rectangular church with a semicircular **apse** and **narthex** copied after the ancient Roman justice hall. It is especially designed for large **congregations**. Also the title given to specific Roman Catholic churches to which the pope has granted particular ceremonial privileges.

- **cathedral.** The chief church of a **diocese** where the **bishop's throne** (or *cathedra*, which is the Latin word for "seat") is situated.
- **collegiate** or **conventual.** A public place of worship served by a community of **regular clergy** (canons regular, **monks**, or friars).
- **metropolitan.** A church presided over by an **archbishop.**
- **parochial.** A *parish* church, with a baptismal **font**, a confessional, and a cemetery, and the liturgical equipment necessary for **baptisms, marriages,** and funerals.

oratory. A place of worship not intended for the use of all the faithful indiscriminately. These can be a public oratory, which is used by a religious community primarily, with limited access by the public; a semipublic oratory, which is intended for use by a special community and is not open to the public; and a private oratory, which is a small **chapel** or a room set apart for worship in a private house for the use of the family or an individual.

OTHER ECCLESIASTICAL STRUCTURES

catacomb. An underground cave or tunnel the early Christians used for burial and as a meeting place during the time of Roman persecutions.

manse. The residence of the clergy, particularly in the Presbyterian Church. May also be called *parsonage, rectory, vicarage,* or *presbytery* (Roman Catholic).

mission. An establishment of **missionaries,** which may include a church, a station, a school, a hospital, and other facilities from which the missionaries do outreach work. May also refer to a local

parish or church that is dependent on a larger church or religious organization for financial support or direction.

shrine. A building or other shelter that encloses the remains or **relics** of a **saint** or other holy person, becoming a site of religious veneration and **pilgrimage**. May also refer to a reliquary or receptacle for sacred relics, or to the niche holding a religious image.

MONASTIC ARCHITECTURE

abbey. A religious house under the direction of an **abbot** or an **abbess**. Also, an abbey church (such as Westminster Abbey).

cell. A small room in a monastery or convent.

cloister. The residence of those who have taken religious vows, such as a convent, monastery, abbey, etc. See also **Sacred Architecture**.

convent. A house for persons under religious vows, in particular, women or **nuns**. May also be called a *nunnery*.

monastery. A house for persons under religious vows, in particular, men or **monks**.

priory. A religious house under the direction of a **prior** or **prioress**.

refectory. The dining room in a monastic community.

retreat house. The guest house at a monastic community.

SACRED ARCHITECTURE
ARCHITECTURAL STYLES

cruciform. Cross-shaped churches, which have a **nave**, **transept**, and **chancel**. When looking down on this formation from above, it would appear to be in the shape of a **Latin cross**.

Gothic. An ornate style of architecture of Europe in the Middle Ages (twelfth to fifteenth centuries). Distinguishing features are pointed arches, ribbed vaulting, and slender spires. Rheims and Notre Dame are Gothic cathedrals.

Romanesque. A style of architecture based on Roman building techniques, prevalent in Europe from the fifth century to the twelfth century. The distinctive features are the round arch and the barrel (or tunnel) vault. It is unadorned and massive.

ARCHITECTURAL FEATURES

bells. The ringing of a church bell is an invitation to worship. If the bells are carillons, sacred **hymn** tunes are played. Bells are tolled for funerals.

•**belfry**. The church tower where the bells are hung.
•**campanile**. A bell tower separate from the church, such as the Leaning Tower of Pisa.
•**carillon**. A set of large bells in the church tower on which **hymn** tunes are played from an electric keyboard. There are at least two octaves of bells, tuned chromatically.

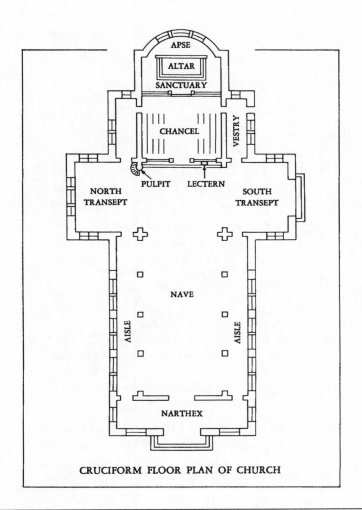

CRUCIFORM FLOOR PLAN OF CHURCH

buttress. An exterior reinforcement to strengthen the walls and support the roof of Gothic style churches. A classic example is Notre Dame Cathedral.

THE CRUCIFORM CHURCH INTERIOR

A view looking east from the nave of a church with a cruciform floor plan.

1. The nave.
2. The pews.
3. The north transept.
4. The south transept.
5. The clerestory.
6. The vaulted ceiling.
7. The lectern.
8. The pulpit.
9. The rood screen.
10. The rood beam.
11. The rood cross.
12. To the chancel area.
13. The choir stalls.
14. The altar rail.
15. To the sanctuary area.
16. The altar.
17. The reredos.
18. The rose window.

cloister. A sheltered corridor connecting the church building with other structures serving the needs of a **congregation**. See also **Monastic Architecture**.

doors. Church doors are often red, dating back to the Middle Ages when church doors were painted red to symbolize the Blood of Christ and to designate the church as a place of sanctuary. Lutheran churches have red doors because the Wittenberg Cathedral, where Martin Luther posted his 95 theses, had red doors. By extension, red doors can signify reformed churches. Some today suggest that the red door means that the mortgage is paid in full!

fleche. (French, "arrow.") A very slender, "arrow-like" **spire** at the **crossing** on a church roof.

gargoyle. Grotesque figure of a person or a beast used as a water spout or decoration on the exterior of a Gothic cathedral. Gargoyles are positioned so that rain water gushes out of their mouths and away from the building. The word *gargoyle* is rooted in the Latin word *gar*, "to swallow," and refers to sound of the water gurgling through these monstrous mouths. Some say gargoyles symbolize the evil that the gospel expels and that they ward off evil spirits.

pier. A support of masonry, steel, or the like for sustaining vertical pressure.

polychrome. Decorative painting in bright colors on wood. Beams in church ceilings, etc., may be ornamented in polychrome.

rose window. A round window with stone **tracery**, generally at the west end of the church.

spire. A steeple projecting high above the roof of the church. Points to heaven, encouraging godly thoughts.

 tracery. Delicately carved stonework that forms the shape of the windows, particularly in Gothic architecture. Such work may also be done in wood on the **chancel** furniture, especially the **reredos.**

vaulted. In Gothic and Romanesque architecture, the domed or arched structure of the ceiling.

MOVING INTO THE CHURCH...
INTERIOR SPACES

It is the doors that admit us to this mysterious place. Lay aside, they say, all that cramps and narrows, all that sinks the mind. Open your heart, lift up your eyes. Let your soul be free, for this is God's temple.
It is likewise the representation of you, yourself. For you, your soul and your body, are the living temple of God. Open up that temple, make it spacious, give it height.
(Romano Guardini)[3]

aisle. The space between the rows of pews that worshipers use as a passageway to reach their places in the **pews.**

apse. (Latin, "arch.") The semicircular or rectangular recess of the **chancel** of a church in which the **altar** stands. The interior of the apse is called the **sanctuary.**

baptistry. This may be a separate building or a part of the church, usually near the entrance, where the sacrament of Holy **Baptism** is administered at a **font.** In some churches it is a large tank in the front of the church for baptism by immersion.

cantoris. The side of the choir where the choir leader or cantor or **precentor** sits. If the altar is on the eastern end, then this would usually be on the north side. For antiphonal singing, the side opposite is called **decani.**

chancel. The **sanctuary** of the church, raised by steps above the level of the **nave.** Separated from the nave by the **rood screen.** Symbolic of heaven or the **Church Triumphant.**

chapel. A small church with a **sanctuary** of its own, either as part of a larger church or separate. It is used for minor and occasional services and functions. A chapel may be connected with an institution such as a college, prison, or cemetery.

choir. The place in the church where the singers sit. May also be called a *choir loft*, especially when set in a gallery behind the pulpit or above the nave. (Also refers to the singers who help with the music of the service.)

clerestory. The upper part of the **nave** containing an arcade of windows. This is a feature of both the basilica and the Gothic-style church.

columns. In cathedrals, the tall columns draw the eye forward to the altar and toward heaven as if in praise to God. There are three traditional styles of columns:

Doric. Plain, unornamented, thick and sturdy, masculine in character. Often used in churches dedicated to male saints.

Ionic. Thinner and more delicate, with the head (or capital) decorated with what looks like opposing scrolls. These columns are viewed as feminine, celebrating wisdom and learning. Often used in churches dedicated to female saints.

Corinthian. The most lavish column, whose capitals are decorated with acanthus leaves and other foliage. Because of their beauty, often used in churches or chapels dedicated to the Virgin Mary.

confessional. In Roman churches, the boothlike structures on either side of the **nave**, in which private confessions are made.

consecration crosses. When a church is consecrated, the bishop makes the sign of the Cross with holy oil three times on each of the church's four walls. The twelve points of this anointing are marked with crosses permanently rendered on the walls with paint or cast in metal or carved in stone. Some churches may have these on the outside walls as well.

crossing. The place at the front of the church where the **transept** and **nave** intersect in a **cruciform** church.

crypt. A vault under a church directly beneath the **sanctuary** or **choir**, used as a chapel or burial place.

decani. The side of the choir opposite the **cantoris** side, normally the south side.

Epistle side. Traditionally, the right side of the **sanctuary** as the **congregation** faces it. This is the side from which the Epistle is read. Also known as the *Epistle Horn*. See also **Gospel side**.

font. (Latin, "fountain.") A round or octagonal receptacle of marble, wood, or metal that stands on a pedestal and contains the water for **baptism**. The number eight signifies regeneration; thus an octagonal font represents regeneration through baptism.

Gospel side. Traditionally, the left side of the **sanctuary** as the **congregation** faces it; the side to the clergy's right. This side is the side of highest honor and from which the Gospel is read. Also known as the *Gospel Horn*. See also **Epistle side**.

horns of the altar. The Epistle side (horn) is the right front as the **congregation** faces the **altar**. The Gospel side (horn) is the left front. The Gospel and Epistle lessons may be read from these positions.

narthex. The vestibule entered by the main entrance and usually stretching across the entire end of the church. It may be under a balcony and is separated from the **nave** of the church by a wall. Today, this is often called a *vestibule*.

nave. (Latin, "ship.") In ecclesiastical art, the Church is represented as a **ship** sailing toward heaven. The ship's "passengers" are the parishioners who sit in the main part of the church, the nave. It extends from the **narthex** to the chancel from which it is separated by a communion rail and sometimes a **rood screen**. The ship (nave) is a symbol of the **Church Militant**, the Church here on earth, the means of our heavenward voyage.

piscina. A basin built into the church wall, having a drain to carry the unused wine from the Eucharist to the ground. A basin with a drain near the altar of a church for disposing of water from liturgical **ablutions**.

portal. Gate or door. The main door of a church or cathedral.

predella. The top step on which the altar stands. Also called *footpace*.

sacristy. A room for the pastor's private use as an office, study, and robing room. A room in a church where sacred vessels and vestments are kept and where the clergy vests. Sometimes called a *vestry*.

sanctuary. The elevated place where the altar stands in the chancel, and where the ordained servant of the **congregation** leads the worship. It is the most sacred part of the church. In nonliturgical churches, may also generally refer to a place where worship services are held.

stall. The special seats in the **chancel** for the clergy. Those for the choir are called *choir stalls*.

transept. In a cruciform church, the area that corresponds to the arms of the cross. It is at the front of the **nave** and at the foot of the **chancel**.

worship center. Not an altar, but a focal point for worship as in a Sunday school room. May be a table with a picture, cross, etc., that suggests worship to those assembled there.

CHURCH FURNISHINGS

ambo. A raised desk, or either of two such desks, from which the Gospels or Epistles are read or chanted. Used especially in an early Christian church or in the Eastern tradition.

bier. The framework upon which a coffin rests.

bishop's throne. Also called the *bishop's chair* or *cathedra*, it is permanently located in a **cathedral**, being placed near the altar on the **Gospel side** of the **sanctuary**.

credence shelf. A shelf or table in the **sanctuary** where the sacramental vessels are kept until carried to the **altar** for the Holy Communion.

lectern. (Latin, "to read.") A wooden or metal desk from which the Bible lessons are read. The lectern may be used instead of the **pulpit** for preaching in lesser services.

pew. A long seat with a back, but without divisions, to accommodate the members of the **congregation** at services. A hymn book rack, pew card holder, communion cup holder, and kneelers may be attached to the pew for the convenience of the worshipers.

presider's chair. The seat on which the presider or **celebrant** sits. Also called *celebrant's chair.*

 prie-dieu. (French, "pray to God.") A movable *prayer desk* with a kneeler for use in services by the clergy or by anyone in **private devotions**. May also be called a *faldstool* or a *litany desk.*

pulpit. (Latin, "raised platform.") The place from which the **sermon** is delivered. It is located at the front of the chancel. It is raised so that the person speaking may be easily seen by the **congregation**. It may be octagonally shaped, symbolic of the regeneration of the spirit by the Word of God.

rood or **rood cross.** (Old English, "cross.") A **cross** or **crucifix**; in particular, a large one at the entrance to the choir or chancel of a medieval church, often suspended on a **rood beam** or **rood screen**.

rood beam. A heavy wooden beam suspended from wall to wall at the entrance to the chancel. On top in the center is a carving or other representation of the crucifixion (**rood**) indicating that humanity must go to heaven by way of the cross.

rood screen. An open screen at the entrance to the sanctuary representing the gates of heaven. The rood screen separates the **nave** from the **chancel**.

sedilia. (Latin, "seat.") Usually a series of three seats for the clergy officiating at a service.

stoup. A small vessel for holding **holy water**, placed at the entrance of a church. Worshipers dip the fingers of the right hand into the holy water and apply it to themselves with the **sign of the cross**, as a blessing and a reminder of **baptism**. Very often the stoup takes the form of a scalloped **shell**.

LITURGICAL FURNISHINGS

alms basin. A large plate into which the offering plates are placed or the offering poured for presentation at the **altar**. Sometimes called a *receiving basin*. May be made of wood, silver, or brass. A velvet pad may be fastened in the bottom.

- **alms bags.** Bags of leather or cloth attached to long poles used to collect the offerings of the people.
- **alms box.** A box placed near the entrance of a church for the collection of financial gifts for the poor or for other specific purposes.
- **offering plates**. Plates of wood or metal used for collecting the offering and then conveying it to the sanctuary. Sometimes wicker baskets are used rather than plates. Offering plates may also be called *collection plates* or *alms plates*.

banners. Large decorated cloths portraying the doctrine and work of the church, to be hung in the church or carried in **procession**.

memorial book. A book listing the memorials given to the glory of God and the church. Also, a book of memory listing the names of those who have served their country in time of war, with special recognition for those who have given their lives. The desk that holds the memorial book is called a **memorial stand**.

parish register. The book in each parish in which all **baptisms**, **confirmations**, funerals, and **marriages** are recorded and in which lists of members are kept. The desk that holds the guest or register book is called a **register stand**.

processional cross. A cross (or **crucifix**) attached to a staff and carried by a **crucifer** at the head of an ecclesiastical **procession**.

register board. Not unlike a hymn board, this one carries such information as the number of members of the parish register, the number present at worship, the amount of the offering, etc. Usually used for the Church School.

sanctuary bracket. A shelf for the **alms basin** and **offering plates** before the offering is received and placed on the **altar**. Usually made of wood, it is attached to the sanctuary wall on the Epistle side.

> *Lift up your heads, O ye gates,*
> *and be ye lifted up, ye everlasting doors,*
> *and the King of Glory shall come in.*

> *Heed the cry of the doors. Of small use to you is a house of wood and stone unless you yourself are God's living dwelling. The high arched gates may be lifted up, and the portals parted wide, but unless the doors of your heart are open, how can the King of Glory enter in?*
> (Romano Guardini)[4]

TWO

The Altar

The altar occupies the holiest spot in the church. The church has itself been set apart from the world of human work, and the altar is elevated above the rest of the church in a spot as remote and separate as the sanctuary of the soul. The solid base it is set on is like the human will that knows that God has instituted man for his worship and is determined to perform that worship faithfully. The table of the altar that rests upon this base stands open and accessible for the presentation of sacrifice. It is not in a dark recess where the actions may be dimly glimpsed, but uncurtained, unscreened, a level surface in plain sight, placed, as the heart's altar should be placed, open in the sight of God without proviso or reservation.

The two altars, one without and the one within, belong inseparably together. The visible altar at the heart of the church is but the external representation of the altar at the center of the human breast, which is God's temple, of which the church with its walls and arches is but the expression and figure. (Romano Guardini)[5]

The altar is the most important furnishing of the church; it is the church's focal point. In fact, a church is built for its altar and not the other way around. At its simplest, the altar is a table of wood or stone from which the **Holy Communion** is consecrated and administered. It is the Lord's Table.

In the early Church the commemoration of the Lord's Supper was part of a bigger meal, and most churches met in private homes, not in public buildings, consecrated or otherwise. So the **Eucharist** was simply administered on an ordinary wooden table used in the home. In the early second century, to honor the memory of those who had died for the faith, the Eucharist was also served on or near the tombs of **martyrs**, with the stone slab that covered the tomb serving as the altar.

It wasn't until the fourth century, after Christians gained the freedom to worship, that permanent altars of wood or stone were erected, as permanent houses of worship were established. Early Christians had carefully avoided using the word "altar" because of its pagan associations, but in the fifth century, references to altars began to appear in construction guidelines. Most stone altars, especially in Rome, stood over the tomb of a **martyr**, and by the early fifth century, a provincial council instructed that only stone altars could be consecrated.

Rules and sensibilities changed over the centuries, with altars in different **rites** taking different forms. But most altars intentionally echo the worship of the early Church by using a wooden altar or a stone altar or a combination of the two. In some large churches, such as cathedrals, both stone and wooden altars are used.

One way the altars combine wood and stone is through the use of a **mensa** (Latin, "table") or *altar stone*, which is a flat stone surface made out of a "single natural stone in one piece and unbreakable." The mensa maybe installed in either a wood or a stone altar. On the top of the *mensa*, five crosses are incised, one in each of the four corners and one in the center. The *mensa* of the altar is covered by the **fair linen**; the **missal** and the Eucharistic vessels are placed on top of the *mensa*, and from here the **Holy Communion** is administered.

Altars today may be permanent or movable, stand against a wall or be freestanding. In general, however, altars face the **congregation**, and the **priest**, whose face was formerly toward the east and whose back was to the nave, now faces the worshipers as well.

In nonliturgical churches, the Communion may be administered from a **communion table** rather than an altar.

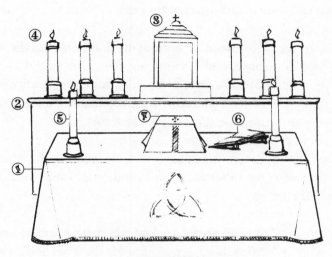

THE ALTAR

1. Altar
2. Gradine
3. Tabernacle
4. Office Lights

5. Altar Lights
6. Missal Stand
7. Veiled Chalice

FURNISHINGS

altar rail. The railing in front of an altar, enclosing the **sanctuary**, that separates the **chancel** from the **nave** of the church. In many churches, worshipers kneel at the altar rail to pray or receive **Holy Communion.** The original function of the altar rail was to keep dogs away from the altar in the early reign of Queen Elizabeth I, when the **rood screen** and **doors** that had separated the nave from the chancel were removed.

altarpiece. A work of art that decorates the space above and behind an altar, such as a *triptych* (Greek, "threefold"), a painting or carving made in three panels, with the outside panels folding over the center one like doors.

gradine. (Latin, "step.") A shelf or table behind the altar on which the cross, the **tabernacle**, and candlesticks may be placed. Also called *retable*.

missal stand. A low wooden or metal, usually brass, book rest that holds the altar book, prayer book, or missal and stands on the *mensa* of the altar.

reredos. An architectural framework of wood, stone, or marble behind and above the altar. It may be embellished with carved figures or other decoration. See also **dossal**.

throne. The elevated step at the back of the altar on which the **cross** stands. It is in the center and slightly higher than the **gradine.**

HANGINGS

baldacchino. A metal, wood, stone, or cloth canopy or dome over the altar or **bishop's throne**. Also called a *canopy*.

dossal. (Latin, "back.") A hanging attached to the wall behind the altar. It is made of a rich fabric and takes the place of a **reredos**. It may hang in fullness or flat against the wall either in one color or the liturgical colors, changing with the seasons of the **Church Year**. Also called a *dorsal*.

riddels. Curtains at each end of the altar, hung on rods supported at the ends by *riddel posts*. Swinging brackets may be used in place of rods.

tester. Not unlike a **baldacchino**, it is a canopy extending over the altar and **predella**. It is flat, and made of wood or fabric.

LIGHTS

> *Our lighted candles are a sign of the divine glory of the one who comes to dispel the dark shadows of evil and to make the whole universe radiant with the brightness of his eternal light. Our candles also show how bright our souls should be when we go to meet Christ.* (Sophronius, seventh century)[6]

The **candles** used in churches bring to mind Jesus' words, "I am the light of the world" (John 9:5). When two candles are used, one on either side of the cross, they represent his two natures, human and divine. Candles on the altar were originally required to be of pure beeswax, but now candles with 51 percent beeswax content or even oil-burning candles are in common usage. Candles may also be called *torches*.

altar lights. The two candles that sit on the altar. They represent the human and divine natures of Christ. Altar lights may be called *eucharistic lights*, *sacramental lights*, or *Gospel lights*. The base of the altar candlesticks may be hexagonal in shape, representing the six attributes of God: power, wisdom, majesty, love, mercy, and justice.

bier lights. Tall candlesticks that stand in the nave beside a coffin during the Burial Office, or funeral. There may be up to six of them, used in pairs. Frequently the **Paschal candle** is also used during funerals.

bishop's candle. An extra single candle placed on the altar or the **gradine** when the **bishop** visits the **parish** and presides at the **Eucharist**.

 candelabra. A branched holder accommodating three, five, or seven candles, representing the **Trinity**, the five wounds of Christ, and the seven gifts of the **Holy Spirit** or the church, respectively. In the Jewish tradition, the seven-branched candelabra is called a *menorah*, representing Old Testament worship, and the nine-branched candelabra is called a *Hanukkah lamp*, commemorating the oil of a single lamp that lasted eight days when the Temple was rededicated during the intertestamental period (cf. John 10:22).

office lights. The candles placed beside or behind an altar and lighted for the **Divine Office**. These candles may be lighted for any service, but are not required, even for the Office. They may be single candles (alone or in groups), a candelabra, or **pavement lights**. Also known as *vesper lights*.

Paschal candle. A large white candle symbolizing the risen Christ. It is placed on the Gospel side of the altar, and is lighted at the **Great Vigil of Easter** on Saturday evening. The Paschal candle burns at all services through **Pentecost** (although formerly it burned only until **Ascension Day**). It may also be lighted for baptismal and funeral services (to symbolize **resurrection**) and may be used as the Christ candle in the center of the **Advent wreath**.

pavement lights. Tall, single candles that usually stand on the floor (pavement) of the sanctuary. These candles are white, and include the candlestick with a candle and stand.

processional torches. Single candles mounted on tall candlesticks carried in processions. Processional torches often double as pavement lights.

sanctuary lamp. A lamp hung in the sanctuary and kept permanently burning with olive oil or beeswax to remind the worshipers of God's presence in the building. In the Roman Catholic Church, the custom eventually grew to burning a candle in front of the **tabernacle** or **aumbry** in which the sacrament is reserved, signifying the presence of God in the **host**.

CANDLE ACCESSORIES

bobeche. Shaped like a small saucer with a hole in the middle, it is placed at the bottom of candles to catch the drippings. It may be made of paper, glass, or metal.

candle burner. To prevent fast burning or gutting of the candles, a metal or glass cap is placed on the top. This "burner" is a sleeve-like cylinder, with the wick of the candle extending through the hole at the top. Also called a *wax-saver* or a *follower*.

candle lighter/extinguisher. A wax taper inside a metal tube with a long wooden handle is used to light the altar candles. Attached is a small metal bell, a snuffer, to extinguish the flame.

LINENS

Linen has much to teach us about the nature of purity. Genuine linen is an exquisite material. Purity is not the product of rude force or found in company with harsh manners. Its strength comes of its fineness. Its orderliness is gentle. But linen is also extremely strong; it is no gossamer web to flutter in every breeze. In real purity there is nothing of that sickly quality that flies from life and wraps itself up in unreal dreams and ideals out of its reach. It has the red cheeks of the man who is glad to be alive and the firm grip of the hard fighter.

And if we look a little further, it has still one thing more to say. It was not always so clean and fine as it now is. It was, to begin with, unsightly stuff. In order to attain its present fragrant freshness it had to be washed and

*rewashed, and then bleached. Purity is not come by at the
first. It is indeed a grace....*

*So the linen on the altar in its fine white durableness
stands to us both for exquisite cleanness of heart and for
fibrous strength.* (Romano Guardini)[7]

Linens are used to cover the altar (**altar linens**) and the sacramental vessels (**sacramental linens**). These linens may be
embroidered, or created out of finely woven **brocades**. Very
often linens will match **vestment** decorations.

ALTAR LINENS

antependium. (Latin, "to hang before.") A silk or other finely
embroidered cloth hung on the front of the **altar**, **pulpit**, and
lectern. The altar antependium may also be called a *frontal*. The
color may be white, green, red, purple, or black.

brocade. A classical material for **paraments** in which the woven
pattern is of ecclesiastical design.

cerecloth. A cloth treated with wax to resist moisture. It is exactly
the size of the *mensa* and is the first cloth placed on the altar,
lying under the **fair linen.**

fair linen. A hand-hemmed cloth of fine linen that covers the top
of the altar and hangs down at each end. It is placed over the **cerecloth** and **antependium**. It is embroidered only in white, with a
cross in each corner and one in the center, representing the five
wounds of Christ, in his hands, his feet, and his side.

frontal. A **parament** that covers the entire front of the altar. See
antependium.

frontlets. Two narrow bands (or *antependia*) hanging over the front of a contemporary altar. May also be called *altar stoles* or *superfrontals*.

paraments. Hangings in the liturgical colors used on the **altar**, **pulpit**, and **lectern**.

second linen. A linen the exact size of the *mensa*, placed on top of the **cerecloth**, to which **frontlets** may be attached.

SACRAMENTAL LINENS

The second type of linens, sacramental linens, are those used for the **Holy Communion**.

book markers. Usually embroidered and fringed ribbon in the liturgical colors used to reserve the pages in the **pulpit** and **lectern** Bibles, and sometimes in the **missal** or altar service book.

burse. A flat stiff envelope covered with silk material in the liturgical color appropriate for the day. The **corporal, pall,** and **chalice veil** are kept in the burse for carrying to and from the altar at the celebration of the **Holy Communion**.

chalice veil. A small cloth that may be embroidered in white to cover the **chalice** only. One of the sacramental linens kept in the burse.

corporal. A square piece of linen about the size of a napkin that is placed on top of the **fair linen** on the altar. On this, the sacramental vessels are placed. The corporal may have one white embroidered cross at the front edge. It symbolizes one of the Lord's grave cloths.

funeral pall. The linen that covers a casket as it is brought into the church for a Christian funeral.

lavabo towel. Used to dry the priest's hands or fingers during the preparatory washing of the hands (**lavabo**) prior to the **Eucharist**. Also used during **baptism** to dry the hands of the priest and the head of the baptized person.

mundatory. A small linen cloth used to wipe the **chalice**, **paten**, and fingers. It is oblong in shape and may be embroidered with a cross in the center.

pall. A piece of cardboard or aluminum about eight inches square, covered with white linen. Usually it has a cross or some other symbol embroidered in white in the center. It is placed over the **chalice**.

purificator. A small rectangular piece of linen used to wipe the edge of the **chalice** as the Communion is administered.

veil. A large square of fine linen used to cover the sacramental vessels. The **chalice** may have its own cover, called the **chalice veil**. It is proper to have crosses embroidered in white on either or both.

HARDWARE

aumbry. A recess in a church wall, especially for holding sacramental vessels.

aspergillum. (Latin, "sprinkler.") The instrument used to sprinkle people and objects with **holy water**, especially in the **Sprinkling Rite** at the beginning of **Mass**.

 **censer.** A container with a cover for burnt **incense** used in worship. As a symbol, it represents the prayers of the faithful which drift upward like incense and present a pleasing aroma to God (Rev. 8:3–5). May be hung on chains. Also called a *thurible* or *incense boat.*

holy water. Water that has been blessed and is used for prayer. It may be used for private prayer, as when entering a church, or in liturgical prayer, as during the **Sprinkling Rite.** Holy water is placed in **fonts** and in **stoups** at the entryways of churches.

incense. The burning of incense is symbolic of prayer, a custom adopted from the Jewish Temple worship (Ps. 141:2). In art, incense also signifies worship and adoration.

> *The offering of an incense is a generous and beautiful rite. The bright grains of incense are laid upon the red-hot charcoal, the censer is swung, and the fragrant smoke rises in clouds. In the rhythm and the sweetness there is a musical quality; and like music also is the entire lack of practical utility: it is a prodigal waste of precious material. It is a pouring out of unwithholding love. . . .*
>
> *The offering of incense is like Mary's anointing at Bethany. It is as free and objectless as beauty. It burns and is consumed like love that lasts through death. And the arid soul still takes his stand and asks the same question: What is the good of it?*
>
> *. . . Incense is the symbol of prayer. Like pure prayer it has in view no object of its own; it asks nothing for itself. It rises like the Gloria at the end of a psalm in adoration and thanksgiving to God for his great glory.*
> (Romano Guardini)[8]

SACRAMENTAL VESSELS

The vessels used for the **Holy Communion**.

chalice. (Latin, "cup.") A metal or ceramic cup used to administer the wine at **Holy Communion**. The classical style is goblet-shaped and made of precious metal. The chalice is representative of the cup used at the Last Supper (1 Cor. 10:16 and 11:25–27).

ciborium. (Greek, "cup.") A companion piece in style and material to the chalice, it contains the bread of the **Holy Communion**. The cover of the cup may be topped with a cross. Also called a *bread box*.

cruet. A small pitcher-like vessel of glass or silver with a stopper; used to hold the wine and water for Communion.

ewer. A vase-shaped pitcher made of silver, pewter, or glass, used to contain the wine and water for Communion.

flagon. Before the wine for **Holy Communion** is consecrated in the chalice, it is kept in a pitcher-like vessel with a lid called a flagon. The wine for Communion may be contained in either a cruet, ewer, or flagon.

host box. Usually a round metal container to hold the wafers for **Holy Communion**.

lavabo. (Latin, "I will wash.") A small metal bowl containing water for washing the fingers of the **celebrant** prior to **Holy Communion** (Ps. 26:6).

monstrance. A transparent container designed to hold the reserved **host** (consecrated wafer) and expose it for adoration. It may be displayed upon the altar or carried in church **procession.** May also be called an *ostensorium.*

paten. (Latin, "dish.") A small dish of precious metal to hold the bread for the **Holy Communion.** The center may be depressed like a saucer.

 pyx. A container made of precious metal used to hold the reserved **host** in the **tabernacles** in the church. A less pretentious one in the shape of a watch-case may be used to carry the **host** to the sick. In art, symbolizes the Last Supper, or the Blessed Sacrament.

repository. In the Roman Catholic Church, a side altar where the **host** is reserved from **Maundy Thursday** until the communion service on **Good Friday.** This special altar is always elaborately decorated. "Repository" may also refer to an enclosed stand that contains the **memorial book.**

sanctus bells. The trio of small bells rung at the singing of the **Sanctus** and at the **consecration** of the bread and wine in the **Eucharist.**

 tabernacle. A small cabinet in which the consecrated elements are kept.

vase. A wooden or metal flower-holder that may be placed on the altar, one at each end of the gradine or between the cross and the candlesticks. It should harmonize in style and material with the cross and candlesticks. Pedestals beside the altar may also accommodate the vases.

While the congregation sings a hymn of thanksgiving or an
appropriate psalm, the celebrant kisses the altar and prays:
Remain in peace, O altar of God, and I hope to return to you
in peace. May the sacrifice which I have offered upon you
forgive my sins, help me to avoid faults and prepare me to
stand blameless before the throne of Christ. I know not
whether I will be able to return to you again to offer sacri-
fice. Guard me, O Lord, and protect your holy church, that it
may remain the way of salvation and the light of the world.
Amen. (Maronite rite)[9]

THREE

The Cross

The cross is the central furnishing of an altar, symbolizing atonement and humankind's redemption. But more than that, the cross is the central symbol of our Christian faith.

Essentially, the cross is a torturous means of criminal execution, analogous to our noose or electric chair. Hard to imagine a hangman's noose or an electric chair as an object of worship and veneration, isn't it? Yet so often we no longer see the suffering, the death, the stench, the terror that is the cross. Dorothy L. Sayers once observed, "It is curious that people who are filled with horrified indignation whenever a cat kills a sparrow can hear the story of the killing of God told Sunday after Sunday and not experience any shock at all."

Looking ahead to his own death, Jesus once told a crowd of Jews and visiting Greek Gentiles, "I, when I am lifted up from the earth, will draw all men to myself" (John 12:32). He understood that it was through the cross that God would be glorified and all people would be reconciled to his holiness. Early Christians realized that following Jesus Christ meant embracing the cross. Paul wrote to the Christians in Galatia, "I have been crucified with Christ and I no longer live, but Christ lives in me" (Gal. 2:20a), and later, "May I never boast except in the cross of our Lord Jesus Christ, through which the world has been crucified to me, and I to the world" (Gal. 6:14). Through this instrument of death has come life, life as it can flow only from God: fresh, vibrant, and unending.

The cross has been transformed, redeemed if you will, from an instrument of destruction into the sign of our glorious King, whom we worship and exalt. This hymn from the Liturgy of St. James acknowledges the profound dichotomy found in the cross of Jesus Christ:

Let all mortal flesh keep silence
And stand with fear and trembling,
Pondering nothing earthly minded,
For the King of kings and Lord of lords comes forth
To be sacrificed and given for food to the faithful.
He is preceded by angels' choirs,
By every Principality and Power,
By the many-eyed Cherubim
And the six-winged Seraphim,
Who cover their faces, chanting:
"Alleluia, Alleluia, Alleluia."[10]

This is not a criminal going to his punishment with the
instrument of his own death laid cruelly on his shoulders,
but the King of kings and the Lord of lords, making a solemn,
royal procession with his cross.

FORMS OF THE CROSS

anchor. The top part is shaped like a cross and the bottom like an anchor, symbolizing Christ as our anchor, our hope. "We have this hope, as an anchor for the soul, firm and secure" (Heb. 6:19).

Budded. A **Latin** or **Greek cross** with trefoil ends representing the **Holy Trinity**. This type is often found at the top of the staff of a Christian flag.

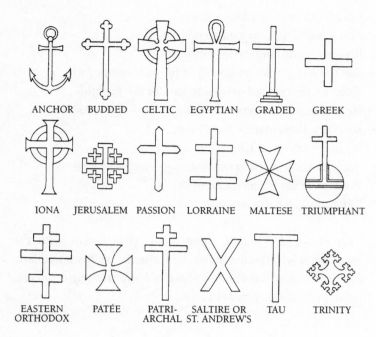

ANCHOR BUDDED CELTIC EGYPTIAN GRADED GREEK

IONA JERUSALEM PASSION LORRAINE MALTESE TRIUMPHANT

EASTERN PATÉE PATRI- SALTIRE OR TAU TRINITY
ORTHODOX   ARCHAL ST. ANDREW'S

Calvary. A **Latin cross** with three steps at the base representing faith, hope, and love, from 1 Corinthians 13:13: "And now these three remain: faith, hope and love. But the greatest of these is love." The cross symbolizes **redemption**, with Christ risen from the dead and reigning from the throne in **heaven**. Sometimes called a *Graded Cross*.

Celtic. Similar to the **Latin cross,** but with a circle signifying eternity surrounding the center of the cross. One of the most ancient of cruciforms, this cross was used by the Celtic Christians in Great Britain and Ireland. Also called the *Irish Cross*, *Cross of Iona*, or *Wheel Cross*.

cross and crown. Symbolizes the reward awaiting the faithful after death (Rev. 2:10).

---

cross and triangle. Used primarily as embroidery on church linen. Represents the unity of Jesus Christ with the **Holy Trinity.**

crosslet. Four **Latin crosses** attached at their bases, representing the spread of Christianity. Often used for **missionary** endeavors.

crucifix. A cross on which there is a representation of the body of Christ. The carved figure of the body of Christ attached to the cross is called the *corpus* (Latin, "body").

Crux Gammata. Also called *croix gammée, swastika,* and *fylfot.* From a pre-Christian Sanskrit form signifying life or health. Though this form has now become a symbol for evil thanks to its association with the Nazi Party and their campaigns of genocide and other atrocities in the Second World War, it is a form found in Christian art through the centuries.

Eastern Orthodox. A cross of early Christianity. Shown with three horizontal bars crossing one vertical bar. The top bar represents the inscription posted by Pilate above the head of Christ and the tilted lower bar represents a footrest. Various explanations are given for the tilted lower bar, but the most likely is that it echoes the cross of Saint Andrew, who is said to have brought Christianity to Russia. (Also called *Byzantine Cross,* the *Eastern Cross,* and the *Russian Orthodox Cross.*)

Egyptian. A cross with a loop at the top like a handle appeared in hieroglyphics and meant "life." It was adopted by the Coptic Christians because Christ is the "Tree of Life." Also called the *ankh* or *"Crux Ansata"* or "cross with handle."

fitchie. Any cross whose lower arm is sharpened. Said to have been used by Crusaders who carried crosses with a pointed lower end so they could be thrust into the ground for devotions.

 fleurie. Four arms of equal length with end caps in the form of a lily, reminding us of the **Resurrection** and of the **Trinity**.

Greek. Four arms of equal length, like a "+" sign. One of the oldest forms of the cross.

Jerusalem. Four **tau crosses** that meet in the center, with a small Greek cross in each of the four corners. The tau crosses are said to represent the Old Testament law, and the small Greek crosses represent the fulfillment of the law in the gospel. Also called a *fivefold* or *Crusader's cross.*

 Latin. An upright cross with the lower portion of the vertical twice as long as the upper part above the crossarm. This was the form of the true cross and, with the Greek Cross, it is one of the oldest forms of the cross.

Lorraine. Similar to the Latin cross, but with two horizontal arms, the longer one being near the base.

Maltese. All the arms are equal in length and broadened at the ends to make two points each, or a total of eight. Its eight points represent the eight **Beatitudes** (Matt. 5:3–10).

 papal cross. Has three horizontal arms, each a little longer than the other, in descending order. This cross is used only in papal **processions**.

passion. The Latin cross with points at the end of each arm, representing the suffering of Christ at his crucifixion.

patée. Similar to the Maltese cross, but with curved arms.

patriarchal. Two horizontal arms on one vertical with the top arm shorter than the second. The upper bar represents the inscription placed on the cross by Pilate. This ecclesiastical cross is carried by the patriarchs in Christian art and **icons** and was adopted by cardinals and **archbishops** as a hierarchical distinction.

Saint Andrew. A leaning cross, shaped like an "X." According to tradition, Saint Andrew felt unworthy to be crucified in the same way as his Lord, so he begged that his cross be made differently. This national cross of Scotland is sometimes called the **Cross Saltire.**

tau. Shaped like the Greek letter "T," which is called a *tau*. Said to be used by early Christians when Christianity was illegal and other forms of the cross could bring unwanted attention. Also called the *anticipatory cross*, for its association with two Old Testament events that anticipate the redemptive work of the Crucifixion: first, the escape of the Israelites from Egypt as the Angel of the Lord passed over the homes that had the cross shape formed by the blood on their doorposts and lintel (Exodus 12); and second, Moses lifting the bronze serpent on a pole to save the people from snake bites (Num. 21:8–9; John 3:14). Often seen in imagery associated with St. Francis of Assisi.

Trinity. Four arms of equal length with three **fleurs-de-lis** at each end.

triumphant (the Cross and Orb). A Latin cross surmounting a globe, symbolizing the final triumph of Christ and his reign over the world. Also called the *Cross of Triumph*, the *Cross of Victory*, and the *Cross of Conquest*.

USES OF THE CROSS

altar cross. On the altar in the church, symbolizing Christ's atonement.

pectoral cross. (From Latin *pectoralis*, "breast.") It is worn on a chain around the neck and rests on the chest over the heart. Originally worn only by **bishops**, it is now commonly used by the **regular clergy**.

pendant. Suspended in the **sanctuary** of a church.

processional. The cross (or crucifix) attached to a staff and carried by a **crucifer** at the head of an ecclesiastical **procession**.

rood. Mounted at the center of the **rood beam**, indicating that the entrance to **heaven** must be by way of the cross.

spire. Proclaiming to all the surrounding community that Jesus is the highest of the high.

> *Now that we have seen the resurrection of Christ, let us adore the all-holy Lord Jesus, the only sinless one. We bow in worship before your cross, O Christ, and we praise and glorify your resurrection, for you are our God, and we have no other, and we magnify your name. All you faithful, come: let us adore the holy resurrection of Christ, for, behold, through the cross joy has come to the world! Let us always bless the Lord, let us sing his resurrection, for by enduring for us the pain of the cross, he has crushed death by his death.* (EASTER SUNDAY PROCLAMATION, ORTHODOX LITURGY)[11]

FOUR

The Liturgical Year

Time, which is now enclosed between the two advents of Christ—his first coming in humility and obscurity, and his second coming in majesty and power—has been claimed by God for his own. Time is to be sanctified like everything else, by the presence and the action of Christ.

The redemption is not simply a past historical fact with a juridical effect on individual souls. It is an ever present reality, living and efficacious, penetrating the inmost depths of our being by the word of salvation and the mystery of faith. The redemption is Christ himself, "who of God is made to us wisdom and justice and sanctification and redemption" (I Cor. 1:30) living and sharing his divine life with his elect. To be redeemed is not merely to be absolved of guilt before God; it is also to live in Christ, to be born again of water and the Holy Spirit, to be in him a new creature, to live in the Spirit.

To say that the redemption is an ever present spiritual reality is to say that Christ has laid hold upon time and sanctified it, giving it a sacramental character, making it an efficacious sign of our union with God in him. So "time" is a medium which makes the fact of redemption present to all men. (Thomas Merton)[12]

DAYS

Day of Humiliation and Prayer. Any specially appointed day set aside for **prayer** and **repentance** by the church or sometimes the government, especially the special services on the last Sunday of the **Trinity Season** inviting the **congregation** to humiliation and repentance. Liturgical color: black.

ember days. Days set aside for **fasting** and **prayer**, namely, the Wednesdays, Fridays, and Saturdays of the weeks following the First Sunday in **Lent; Pentecost;** September 14; and the Third Sunday in **Advent**.

octave. A period of eight consecutive days that extends the time a **solemnity** is celebrated. The Christian year has two octaves. One is the Octave of **Christmas**, which lasts from December 25 to January 1 with the Solemnity of Mary the Mother of God. The second is the **Easter** Octave, which begins on Easter Sunday and ends on the Second Sunday of Easter, or Low Sunday. In addition, **Pentecost** Sunday concludes the great octave of eight weeks which is the Season of Easter.

Sabbath. Most correctly, the seventh day of the week or Saturday, the day on which God rested after creation (Gen. 2:2–3) and the day that he commanded be honored as a day of rest by the Jews (Exod. 20:8–11). Sometimes *Sabbath* is used to designate the day of Christian worship, **Sunday.**

Sunday or the **Lord's Day.** The first day of the week, and the weekly commemoration of Christ's **Resurrection** on that day (John 20:1–25). From the earliest days of the Church, Christians gathered on the first day of the week (Acts 20:7; 1 Cor. 16:2), as well as on the seventh day (or the **Sabbath**). But as the gentile influence increased in the Church, gradually the observation of the Jewish **Sabbath** waned. "The Lord's Day" is first used in the Book of Revelation (1:10).

CHURCH YEAR

Also called the *liturgical year* or the *ecclesiastical year*. The Church Year is arranged into two large divisions, first the festival portion commemorating the life and work of Jesus Christ, and second, the nonfestival portion, setting forth the standards of the Christian life.

SEASONS OF THE CHURCH YEAR

Christ has given a special meaning and power to the cycle of the seasons, which of themselves are "good" and by their very nature have a capacity to signify our life in God: For the seasons express the rhythm of natural life. They are the systole and diastole of the natural life of our globe. Jesus has made this ebb and flow of light and darkness, activity and rest, birth and death, the sign of a higher life, a life which we live in him, a life which knows no decline, and a day which does not fall into darkness. It is the "day of the Lord" which dawns for us anew each morning, the day of Easter, the "eighth day," the Pascha Domini, *the day of eternity, shining upon us in time.* (Thomas Merton)[13]

The five seasons of the church year are **Advent**, **Christmas** (Christmas through the Baptism of Our Lord), **Lent**, the **Paschal Triduum** (a three-day season that begins at sundown **Holy Thursday** and may end either at the **Easter Vigil** or at sundown **Easter Sunday**), and **Easter** (Easter through **Pentecost** Sunday).

The time of the year not associated with the five seasons of the church year is known as **Ordinary Time** (from the Latin word *ordinal*, meaning "counted"). Each week of Ordinary Time is assigned a number, and these weeks are divided into two groups. The first group (sometimes called "Ordinary Time 1") is that which falls between the seasons of Christmas and Lent. In the Anglican and **Protestant** traditions, this season is known as the season of **Epiphany**.

The second group (sometimes called "Ordinary Time 2") begins with **Trinity Sunday** (the Sunday after **Pentecost** Sunday) and runs through the **Feast of Christ the King** (the last Sunday of the church year). This season is sometimes known as the *Trinity Season* and in the Anglican and **Protestant** traditions, may be known as the season of **Pentecost**.

CYCLES OF THE CHURCH YEAR

What exactly is a feast day? Just as one can say that an altar is a piece of earth raised a little towards heaven, so one can say of a feast day that it is a piece of time which touches eternity. (Joseph Jungmann)[14]

The church year is also divided into cycles: The **Temporal Cycle** (*Temporale*) divides the church year into three seasons that celebrate the entire mystery of redemption: The Christmas Cycle (**Advent** and **Christmas** season), the Easter Cycle (**Lent**, the **Triduum**, and **Easter** season), and **Ordinary Time**. The **Sanctoral Cycle** (*Sanctorale*) includes the holy days and saints' days. **Holy days** honor specific events from the Scriptures; **saints' days** honor specific people or saints.

There are a number of ways to categorize the special days we observe in the church year. Sometimes we use the simple designations of **feasts** or **fasts**.

- **fast.** (Anglo-Saxon, "to observe.") To go without food for religious reasons. The seasons of **Lent** and **Advent** are penitential seasons of fasting. At one time there were numerous fasts in the Church calendar, but after the reforms of Vatican II, fast days have been reduced to **Ash Wednesday** and **Good Friday**.

- **feast.** (Latin, "joyful.") Same as *festival*. Days of religious celebration. Sundays are always feast days because they commemorate the **Resurrection**. The Major Feasts are those honoring God, and the Minor Feasts are those remembering saints.
- *feria.* An ordinary weekday, neither feast nor fast. Refers also to plain or simple music appropriate for days without special observance.
- **festal.** Pertaining to a feast or festival. Also the more elaborate music appropriate to a feast or festival.

Another designation used in describing the church year is **moveable** and **immovable feasts**:

- **movable feasts** (or fasts). Holy days, the dates of which are regulated by the date of **Easter**, thereby varying from year to year, such as **Ash Wednesday**, **Good Friday**, **Pentecost**.
- **immovable feasts.** Those days that always fall on the same date, such as **Christmas**, **Epiphany**, and **saints' days**.

Yet another designation that was once used for the church year is red-letter days and black-letter days, terms derived from an interesting practice:

- **red-letter days.** The most important days celebrated in the church year, printed in red ink in the ecclesiastical calendar. In general, these were celebrations that had their own **Propers** (**collect**, Epistle, **Gradual**, and Gospel).
- **black-letter days.** The feasts and fasts that were less important, and therefore printed in black ink in the ecclesiastical calendar.

The most recent changes in the Roman calendar, made following Vatican II, apply the designations of **solemnities**, **feasts**, and **memorials** to holy days and saints' days.

- A **solemnity** is the most important of days, a principal day that eclipses all other days of the church year. Solemnities include Sundays, **Christmas**, and **Easter**.
- A **feast** is less important than a solemnity, but more important than a memorial.
- A **memorial** commemorates a saint or blessed (one beatified, but not yet canonized), and is not celebrated in the week before **Christmas**, **Holy Week**, or **Easter Week**.

COLORS OF THE CHURCH YEAR

It is as if one strong dazzling beam of light shone down upon us from the risen Lord; this beam is refracted and diffused for our weak eyes through the spectrum of the Church year. Just as we cannot see the richness of the colors contained in a single beam of sunlight unless it is sent through a prism, so too the Church year shows us all the different aspects, all the richness and glory of the one, central, all-embracing, unifying event of the Lord's death and resurrection, which we call the paschal mystery, which we celebrate in the Eucharist.

For this reason the Church has her different seasons, her variety of feasts; for this reason she celebrates the death and resurrection of the Lord in so many different ways: at Easter and in Holy Week, in the Ascension and at Pentecost, at Christmas and Epiphany, in Advent and Lent, in the other feasts of the Lord, in those of his mother, and of his saints. The Church year is a precious diamond in the hands of our mother the Church; slowly she turns it around, so that we may see every facet, every aspect of it. It is one stone— Easter—with many facets: all the feasts. (John Shea)[15]

Liturgical colors change with the seasons of the ecclesiastical year and serve as visual reminders of the nature of the season being celebrated. The colors appropriate to the season appear in the **paraments** on the **altar**, **pulpit**, and **lectern** and in the **celebrant's stole**, **maniple**, and **chasuble**. The colors may vary according to the tradition. Below are the colors in the Roman tradition, with variations noted.

black. Signifying mourning and death, black is used in **Masses** and **offices of the dead**, and on **All Souls Day**. In the Anglican tradition, it may be used on **Ash Wednesday** and **Good Friday** as well.

blue. The color of hope, blue is used in the Anglican tradition as an alternative to the liturgical purple in the season of **Advent**. Often called *Sarum blue* from its use in the medieval Sarum Rite (Salisbury, England). Blue is associated also with the **Virgin Mary**, and some churches use blue on her feast days.

gold. May be used instead of **white** as the liturgical color on **Easter** to give emphasis to the most holy day of the church year. It is also appropriate for the Last Sunday after Pentecost, the **Feast of Christ the King**, as well as on other occasions on which white is used.

green. The liturgical color of **Ordinary Time**, symbolizing life and growth.

purple or **violet.** The liturgical color symbolizing penitence and mourning, used during the two penitential seasons, **Advent** and **Lent**. Also used in **Masses for the Dead** and funeral Masses.

red. The liturgical color symbolizing love and zeal, bringing to mind fire and blood. It is used on **Palm Sunday**, **Good Friday**, and for celebrations of the **Passion**. It is also appropriate for feasts of **apostles**, **evangelists**, and **martyrs**. It is also used on **Pentecost**, the day on which the **Holy Spirit** descended, appearing in tongues of fire, and since recognized as the birthday of the Christian Church. As such it is used for **ordinations**, conventions of the church, and dedications and anniversaries of the Church and **congregations**. It is also appropriate for the feast days of saints who were **martyrs**. Crimson may used during **Holy Week** in Anglican churches.

rose or **pink.** Used to signal joy in reaching the midway point in the penitential season, this color may be used as an optional alternative to purple only on the Third Sunday of **Advent** (*Gaudete* Sunday) and on the Fourth Sunday of **Lent** (*Laetare* Sunday).

white. The liturgical color symbolizing purity and joy. It is used at **Christmas** and **Easter** and the non-Passion feasts of the Lord; for the feasts of Mary (**The Presentation, The Annunciation, The Visitation**); for non-martyred **saints**, such as Saint John; and for **angels**, such as Saint Michael. White may also be used for funerals or funeral Masses, especially in the funerals of children. In the Anglican church, white is often used for baptisms and weddings as well.

TEMPORAL CYCLE
(THE PROPER OF TIME)

THE ADVENT SEASON

Advent. (Latin, "coming.") The first season of the Church Year, which begins with the fourth Sunday before **Christmas**. The first Sunday is called Advent Sunday. A period of preparation for the coming of the Lord at Christmas and at the end of time, it lasts about four weeks, ending at Christmas. Liturgical color: purple.

SYMBOLS OF THE ADVENT SEASON

Advent calendar. Especially appropriate for children, the calendar has numbered "doors," one to be opened daily in anticipation of **Christmas**. Behind each "door" is a suitable picture.

Advent candles. Symbolize the anticipated approach and ultimate birth of Jesus Christ as the Light of the World. Generally, four candles representing the weeks in Advent are used: The first is the Prophecy Candle, the second the  Bethlehem Candle, the third the Shepherd's Candle, and the fourth the Angel's Candle. A taller candle, the Christ Candle, placed in the center, is lighted last, on Christmas Eve. The four Advent candles may all be white or all violet, or they may consist of three violet candles and one rose candle (to be lit on the third Sunday). Sarum blue candles may be used instead of violet in churches whose linens in Advent are Sarum blue. Often the Advent candles are placed within an unadorned wreath of evergreen called the **Advent wreath**.

Advent rose. A symbol of the Messianic hope adopted in the thirteenth century from a small, colorful Palestinian rose.

O antiphons. The antiphons sung at **Vespers** on the seven nights preceding Christmas Eve (December 17–23), so-called because each antiphon begins with the word "O": *O Sapientia* (O Wisdom); *O Adonai* (O Lord); *O Radix Jesse* (O Root of Jesse); *O Clavis David* (O Key of David); *O Oriens* (O Dayspring); *O Rex Gentium* (O King of the Gentiles); and *O Emmanuel*. Forms of these antiphons comprise the verses of the familiar Advent hymn "O Come, O Come, Emmanuel."

THE CHRISTMAS SEASON

Christ is born. He is born to us. And, he is born today. For Christmas is not merely a day like every other day. It is a day made holy and special by a sacred mystery. It is not merely another day in the weary round of time. Today, eternity enters into time, and time, sanctified, is caught up into eternity. Today, Christ, the eternal Word of the Father, who was in the beginning with the Father, in whom all things were made, by whom all things consist, enters into the world which he created in order to reclaim souls who had forgotten their identity. Therefore, the Church exults, as the angels come down to announce not merely an old thing which happened long ago, but a new thing which happens today. (Thomas Merton)[16]

Christmas. Christmas (Christ's Mass) is one of the major festivals of the Christian Year, celebrated on December 25 and commemorating the birth of Christ. This feast is a celebration of the **Incarnation**, when God became human. Also called the *Nativity of Our Lord*. Liturgical color: white.

SYMBOLS OF THE CHRISTMAS SEASON

angels. Heavenly beings who feature largely in the story of the birth of Jesus. Angels appear to Mary, to Joseph, to the shepherds, and to the **Magi**, guiding, warning, filling the skies with music and the viewers with wonder. Angels appear on other occasions in Scripture, but are especially associated with Christmas. See also **St. Michael and All Angels.**

archangel. An angel of higher rank. The archangel Gabriel announced the births of both John the Baptist and Jesus, and is shown with a right arm raised in announcement. See also the **Annunciation.**

bambino. The figure of the Infant Jesus.

Christmas rose. A white rose (*Helleborus niger*) that blooms in winter, symbolizing the purity of the **Virgin Mary** and the Child Jesus.

crèche. (French, "crib.") A three-dimensional scene of the Nativity with the Holy Infant in his "crib." Also includes representations of Jesus in a manger, with Mary and Joseph attending him, while the animals in the stable, the shepherds, and the **Magi** gather to worship. Sometimes the manger is shown by itself, symbolic of the entire story.

The Holy Family of Jesus, Mary, and Joseph. The Sunday after Christmas (within the Octave of Christmas). A time to honor the family of Jesus.

Jesse tree. A tree stump from which a branch shoots out, symbolizing Isaiah's prophecy (11:1) foretelling a promised **Messiah**, who would come through Jesse, the father of King David. The Nativity accounts of Matthew and Luke each include a lineage that traces the line of Jesus back to David. Sometimes this is called a *branch (of Jesse)*.

star. Reminder of the star that later led the **Magi** to the Holy Child.

The Twelve Days of Christmas. The season of Christmas, from Christmas Day (December 25) through Epiphany (January 6), a time of joy, relaxation, and hospitality. The evening of January 5 is sometimes called *Twelfth Night*, a night anticipating Christ's **Epiphany**.

THE EPIPHANY OF OUR
LORD JESUS CHRIST

Sometimes called *Twelfth Day*. January 6, the final and grandest
day of the Christmas season, the day on which the Wise Men from
the East, following a star and bearing gifts for royalty, made their
way to Bethlehem to worship the king (Matt. 2:1–12). The word
"Epiphany" is Greek, meaning "to show forth" or "manifestation."
This glorious festival celebrates the manifestation of God to the
Gentiles as well as two other great manifestations of God: in the
descending dove and the voice affirming Christ's identity after
his baptism (Matt. 3:13–17), and the miraculous transformation
of water into wine at the wedding at Cana (John 2:1–11).
Liturgical color: white.

> *In choosing to be born for us, God chose to be known by us.
> He therefore reveals himself in this way, in order that this
> great sacrament of his love may not be an occasion for us of
> great misunderstanding.*
>
> *Today the magi find, crying in a manger, the one they
> have followed as he shone in the sky. Today the magi see
> clearly, in swaddling clothes, the one they have long awaited
> as he lay hidden among the stars.*
>
> *Today the magi gaze in deep wonder at what they see:
> heaven on earth, earth in heaven, humanity in God, God in
> humanity, one whom the whole universe cannot contain now
> enclosed in a tiny body. As they look, they believe and do not
> question, as their symbolic gifts bear witness: incense for God,
> gold for a king, myrrh for one who is to die. . . .*
>
> *Today Christ enters the Jordan to wash away the sin of
> the world. John himself testifies that this is why he has come:
> Behold the Lamb of God, behold him who takes away the
> sins of the world. . . .*

Today Christ works the first of his signs from heaven by turning water into wine. But water [mixed with wine] has still to be changed into the sacrament of his blood, so that Christ may offer spiritual drink from the chalice of his body. (Peter Chrysologus)[17]

SYMBOLS OF EPIPHANY

frankincense. A gift of the **Magi** at the cradle of the Christ Child, an incense to honor God come as a child.

gold. A gift of the **Magi** to the Christ Child, signifying his royalty.

Magi. The visitors from the East who followed the star to find the Holy Family. They worshiped the Child and presented gifts of gold, frankincense, and myrrh. Sometimes "Magi" is rendered Wise Men or Kings, but they are generally considered likely to be astrologers from Persia or Arabia.

myrrh. An aromatic gum resin symbolizing suffering because of its bitterness; also used in Christ's burial. This gift of the **Magi** foreshadowed the death of Jesus Christ.

pyramid and star. This symbol represents the flight of the **Holy Family** into Egypt.

THE BAPTISM OF OUR LORD

The first Sunday after Epiphany, celebrating John's baptism of Jesus in the Jordan River (Matt. 3:13–17; Mark 1:9–11; Luke 3:21–22; John 1:29–34).

ORDINARY TIME 1

Also called the *Season after Epiphany* in the Anglican and **Protestant** traditions. The time between **Christmas/Epiphany** and **Ash Wednesday,** beginning the Monday after the **Baptism of Our Lord** and ending on **Shrove Tuesday.** Liturgical color: Green.

PRE-LENTEN SEASON

Prior to calendar revisions in 1969, this three-week season was a preparation for **Lent,** which in turn was a preparation for **Easter.** The Sundays of Quinquagesima, Sexagesima, and Septuagesima have recently been dropped from the Church calendar, although references to these Sundays appear still in devotional readings and older liturgical writings. Liturgical color: purple (as Lent) or green (as Ordinary Time).

- **Septuagesima.** (Latin, "seventieth.") The Sunday that is approximately seventy days before Easter.
- **Sexagesima.** (Latin, "sixty.") The Sunday nearest sixty days before Easter.
- **Quinquagesima**. (Latin, "fiftieth.") The Sunday before **Ash Wednesday**, approximately fifty days before Easter.

Carnival. (from the Latin, "removal of meat") or **Mardi Gras**. The unofficial season of exaggerated decadence, recklessness, and make-believe, before entering **Lent**, the time of penitence and reflection. When Carnival begins is unclear, but it always ends on the Tuesday before **Ash Wednesday**.

Shrove Tuesday. The Tuesday before **Ash Wednesday.** The day to make confession to shriveners (priests) and thus be "shriven" (absolved of sin) in preparation for Lent. Also the day to use up milk, eggs, butter, and meats: foods that are either forbidden or restricted during Lent. So this day may be known as *Pancake Tuesday, Fat Tuesday*, or *Butter Tuesday*.

LENT

Now we can understand why the church has at heart to cleanse herself from the filth that adheres to her garment from the sins of Christians. The soap, the lye, and the broom used by the church for this cleansing process is fasting.

The dust and dirt accumulated over winter have to be routed. Outside in the gardens, now at the coming of spring, leaves and dry grass have to be raked together and burned. Now in the time of Lent, Mother Church, too, like the house-wife and the gardener, is determined to burn up and to rout the dust and trash of our sins. The means she employs are fasting, mortification, abstinence, and self-conquest.
(Pius Parsch)[18]

A season of **prayer**, **fasting**, and penitence in preparation for **Easter**. Historically, Lent is the time when catechumens are prepared for **baptism** at the **Easter Vigil**.

The season begins on **Ash Wednesday**, a movable date, and lasts for forty days. The forty days of Lent are counted in two fashions. The first counts **Ash Wednesday** as day one, with the last day being **Holy Saturday** (46 days). The six Sundays are omitted from the counting as these are celebrations of Christ's **Resurrection** and so are exempt from the mourning of Lent; (omitting them results in forty days). The second method is to reckon **Ash Wednesday** and the following Thursday, Friday, and Saturday as a preview of Lent, then begin the count of forty days on the first Sunday in Lent, with the last day falling on **Maundy Thursday**. In this reckoning, **Good Friday**, **Holy Saturday**, and **Easter Sunday** comprise the **Paschal Triduum**.

Traditionally, the fifth Sunday in Lent was called Passion Sunday. It opened the two-week season of *Passiontide*, which encompassed the fifth week of Lent, the sixth Sunday (**Palm Sunday**), and **Holy Week**, which followed. Today, Passion Sunday is the sixth week of Lent, superseding the name of **Palm Sunday**, although both a Liturgy of the Palms and a Liturgy of the Passion may be celebrated. Popularly, this Sunday is still known as **Palm Sunday**.

Lent may be called *Passion Season*, from the Latin, *passio*, or suffering, recalling Christ's spiritual suffering during **Holy Week** (the betrayal by his friends, their Last Supper, his prayer in Gethsemane, and his arrest and trial) and his physical suffering on the cross on **Good Friday**. During this season, the "**Alleluia**" is omitted completely from all liturgy, buried and awaiting the **resurrection** of Easter. Liturgical color: purple or Lenten array, a natural-colored linen bordered in purple and red or black and red.

ASH WEDNESDAY

The name is taken from the custom of putting ashes on the forehead on this first day of Lent, as a reminder of our need for **repentance**. The date of Ash Wednesday depends on the date of Easter, because it always falls forty-six days before Easter. The ashes used are the powdered ashes of the burnt palms of the previous year's **Palm Sunday**.

> . . . *all this flourishing life, turns to a little ash, a handful of dry dust, which every breeze scatters this way and that. All this brilliant color, all this sensitive, breathing life, falls into pale, feeble, dead earth, and less than earth, into ashes. It is the same with ourselves. We look into an opened grave and shiver: a few bones, a handful of ash-grey dust.*
>
> *Remember man*
> *that dust thou art*
> *and unto dust shalt thou return.*

Ashes signify man's overthrow by time. Our own swift passage, ours and not someone else's, ours, mine. When at the beginning of Lent the priest takes the burnt residue of the green branches of the last Palm Sunday and inscribes with it on my forehead the sign of the cross, it is to remind me of my death.

    Memento homo
    quia pulvis est
    et in pulverem reverteris.

Everything turns to ashes, everything whatever.
(Romano Guardini)[19]

THE SUNDAYS OF LENT

- **Invocavit.** The first Sunday in Lent, named from the first word of the **introit** in Latin: *Invocavit me, et ego exaudiam eum,* "He shall cry to me and I will hear him." Sometimes this Sunday may be called **Quadragesima**, from the Latin for "fortieth," as it falls forty days before Easter.
- **Reminiscere.** (Latin, "remember.") This is the second Sunday in Lent. The name is derived from the first Latin word of the **introit**: *Reminiscere miserationum tuarum, Domine,* "Be mindful, O Lord, of Thy compassions and Thy mercy."
- **Oculi.** The third Sunday in Lent. Its name is given by the first Latin word of the **introit**: *Oculi mei semper ad Dominum,* "My eyes are ever on the LORD" (Ps. 25:15).
- **Laetare.** (Latin, "rejoice.") The fourth Sunday in Lent, from the opening words of the **introit**: *Laetare, Jerusalem: et conventum facite,* "Rejoice, O Jerusalem, and come together." Also known as Mothering or Refreshment Sunday. The colors may be changed from purple to rose or violet for this Sunday.
- **Judica.** The fifth Sunday in Lent. The name comes from the first word of the **introit** in Latin: *Judica me, Deus,* "Vindicate me, O God" (Ps. 43:1). Prior to the 1969 calendar reform, this day was known also as Passion Sunday, marking the

beginning of Passiontide, which included Passion Week and **Holy Week**.

Palm Sunday (or *Palmarum*). The sixth Sunday in Lent and the first day of **Holy Week**. It commemorates Christ's Triumphal Entry into Jerusalem (Matt. 21:1–11; Mark 11:1–11; Luke 19:28–40; John 12:12–19). May also be called *Passion Sunday* or *Sunday of the Passion*.

 **palm** (or *palm branch*). A sign of victory, used in Christ's Triumphal Entry into Jerusalem (see Ps. 118:26–27). Palms are often used to decorate churches on Palm Sunday and are distributed to worshipers as part of the worship service.

All glory, laud, and honor
To thee, Redeemer King:
To whom the lips of children
Made sweet hosannas ring.
(Theodulph)[20]

HOLY WEEK

Holy Week is the week before Easter. On Palm Sunday, Christ made his triumphal entry into Jerusalem. On Monday and Tuesday he taught in the Temple. On Wednesday, he rested at Bethany. On Thursday, he returned to Jerusalem, ate the Last Supper with his disciples, and was betrayed by Judas. On Friday, he was crucified, and on Saturday, his body lay in the tomb. Sometimes called *Passion Week*.

To do justice to the mystery of Easter joy with the stale words
of human speech is rather difficult. This is so not only
because every mystery of the Gospel penetrates only with

difficulty into the narrow confines of human life—thereby making it even harder for our words to grasp and contain and express these mysteries—but because the Easter message is the most human tidings of Christianity. That is why we find it the most difficult message to understand. For what is most true, most obvious, and most easy, is the most difficult to be, to do, and to believe. That is to say, modern people base life on the unexpressed, and therefore all the more self-evident, prejudice that anything "religious" is merely an affair of the most interior heart and of the loftiest spirit—something that we must bring about by ourselves, something, therefore, that involves the difficulties and unreality of the heart's thoughts and moods.

But Easter tells us that God has done something. God himself. And his action has not merely gently touched the heart of a person here and there, so that they tremble slightly from an ineffable and nameless someone. God has raised the Son from the dead. God has quickened the flesh. God has conquered death. God has done this—he has conquered—not merely in the realm of inwardness, in the realm of thought, but in the realm where we, the glory of the human mind notwithstanding, are most really ourselves: in the actuality of this world, far from all "mere" thoughts and "mere" sentiments. He has conquered in the realm where we experience practically what we are in essence: children of the earth, who die. (Karl Rahner)[21]

THE PASCHAL TRIDUUM

Begins at sundown on Maundy Thursday and ends at sundown on Easter Sunday.

Maundy Thursday (or **Holy Thursday**). The Thursday of Holy Week when Christ washed the feet of his disciples, instituted the

Lord's Supper, and gave a new commandment of love. The name is derived from the Gospel reading from John 13:34: *Mandatum novum do vobis*, "A new command I give you: Love one another." Liturgical color: purple, red, or Lenten array, although white may be used if the service is one of **Holy Communion.**

tenebrae. (Latin, "darkness.") During services on the last three days of Holy Week, the candles and lights of the church are gradually extinguished until the church is in total darkness, reminiscent of the darkness that covered the earth at the Crucifixion. Psalm 51 is often sung at this time.

Good Friday. The Friday in Holy Week, the week before **Easter**. The day on which the Crucifixion is commemorated. Liturgical color: black.

The Three Hours. A service held on Good Friday from 12:00 noon until 3:00 PM, commemorating the Crucifixion. A common meditation at this service is the *Seven Last Words of Christ* from the cross:

- "Father, forgive them, for they do not know what they are doing." (Luke 23:34);
- "I tell you the truth; today you will be with me in paradise." (Luke 23:43);
- "Dear woman, here is your son," and "Here is your mother." (John 19:26, 27);
- "My God, my God, why have you forsaken me?" (Matt. 27:46, Mark 15:34);
- "I am thirsty." (John 19:28);
- "It is finished." (John 19:30);
- "Father, into your hands I commit my spirit." (Luke 23:46).

Holy Saturday. The day before Easter Sunday, when Christ's body lay in the tomb.

Easter Vigil. Considered the "mother of all vigils," it begins after nightfall on Holy Saturday and ends before dawn on Easter. This vigil includes extensive readings from Scripture, psalms, prayers, and the lighting of the **Paschal candle**.

SYMBOLS OF CHRIST'S PASSION

cock or **rooster.** Indicates watchfulness. A passion symbol representing Peter, who denied Jesus three times before the cock crowed on the morning of Jesus' crucifixion (Mark 14:72).

coins. See **money bag** (below).

crown of thorns. The Roman soldiers plaited a crown of thorns and mockingly placed it upon Jesus' head. Sometimes shown with a **cross**.

dice. A passion symbol of our Lord, representing the casting of lots for his seamless robe (John 19:23–24). Sometimes shown with a coat or robe.

ewer and basin. A passion symbol representing Pilate, who washed his hands as a sign that he was not guilty of Christ's blood (Matt. 27:24–26). Sometimes shown with a towel.

INRI. The title written by Pilate and nailed at the top of the cross. These are the initial letters of the Latin inscription, *Iesus Nazarenus Rex Iudaeorum*, "Jesus of Nazareth, King of the Jews" (Matt. 27:37; Mark 15:26; Luke 23:38; John 19:19).

ladder. A passion symbol often pictured with a reed and sponge, articles used in the crucifixion.

money bag. With thirty pieces of silver, the money bag represents Judas who betrayed our Lord for the money, but seeing what he had done, returned it in remorse (Matt. 26:14–16; 27:3–8).

nails. Three nails, sometimes shown with a crown of thorns, are a passion symbol of our Lord. The story of the Crucifixion does not mention the use of nails, but we get this information from Thomas after the **Resurrection** when he asked to feel the wounds made by the nails (John 20:25).

robe. A scarlet or purple robe with a reed is a passion symbol of our Lord (Matt. 27:28; Mark 15:17).

rope. A symbol of the Passion because Jesus was bound at his arrest (John 18:12) and when taken to Pilate the following morning (Matt. 27:2; Mark 15:1). Also the instrument of Judas' suicide (Matt. 27:5).

 scourge. A passion symbol. Christ was scourged (flogged) after his trial, and before he was led to Calvary (Matt. 27:26; Mark 15:15; John 19:1).

spear and sponge. Articles used at the crucifixion to provide Jesus with wine while on the cross and therefore passion symbols of our Lord (Matt. 27:34, 48; Mark 15:23; John 19:29, 34; see also Ps. 69:21). Sometimes shown as a reed and sponge, or with a ladder.

torch. An emblem of the betrayal by Judas (John 18:3).

EASTER DAY

Alleluia! Christ is risen!
Christ is risen indeed! Alleluia![22]

On this "Queen of the Festivals" of the church year, we commemorate the **Resurrection** of our Lord. In the early Church, the celebration of the Resurrection of Jesus was associated with the Jewish Passover and even today retains this association in the words of the liturgy. Indeed, throughout most of the non-English speaking world, this celebration is known as *Pascha*, or *Pasch* from the Greek for Passover. Like the Jewish Passover, the date of Easter is variable and all other movable feasts are dependent upon it. Easter occurs the first Sunday after the first full moon after the vernal equinox, March 21. The English word *Easter* derives from an Anglo-Saxon spring goddess called *Eostre* (according to the writings of the Venerable Bede), whose old pagan festival Easter replaced. Also called *Resurrection Sunday*. Liturgical colors: white and gold.

SYMBOLS OF EASTER

butterfly. A symbol of the **Resurrection**, as a caterpillar disappears into a cocoon (grave) only to emerge as a butterfly.

dolphin. Early believers were met with opposition and persecution from both civil and religious authorities. It became critical to keep one's beliefs and allegiances as private as possible, so as not arouse suspicion of the authorities. For this reason, the early Church adopted many of its images and symbols from pagan sources and simply imbued them with Christian meaning. In classical mythology, the dolphin was thought to carry souls to the islands of the dead, and became associated with the idea of **resurrection**, an idea that the early Church kept when it included the dolphin as one of its symbols. The dolphin is also associated with **fish**, a common and popular symbol in the early Church.

lily. The Easter lily symbolizes the **Resurrection**, as a glorious flower emerging from a seemingly dead bulb (grave).

passion flower. A flower used as the symbol of the suffering of Jesus. Its ten petals are said to represent the ten Apostles; Peter, for his denial, and Judas, for his betrayal, are not included. The five stamens remind us of the five wounds; the three styles of the three nails; the leaf of the spear; and the tendrils of the cords. This flower is woven into damask fabrics or embroidered on purple **paraments**.

peacock. In the mythology of imperial Rome, the peacock was Juno's sacred bird and symbolized immortality. Adopted by the early Church, the peacock remained a symbol of eternal life, and specifically, the Resurrection of Christ. It is sometimes shown drinking from a sacramental **chalice**.

pelican or **pelican-in-her-piety.** The symbol of the pelican shows the bird on its nest pecking open its own breast to feed its young with its blood, recalling Christ's wound on the Cross that flowed with blood and water. Because of its self-sacrifice, the pelican has become a symbol of Christ's **atonement** for humanity. The source of the image is found in the King James Version of Ps. 102:6: "I am like a pelican of the wilderness. . . . "

phoenix. According to ancient myth, this large bird of great beauty lived to be between three and five hundred years old and then set its nest on fire and was consumed by the flames. Out of the ashes came a new live bird, restored to its youth, to begin another life cycle. The phoenix was introduced to the early Church by Saint Clement, who used it as an image of the **resurrection** of the dead and the triumph of eternal life over death, ultimately becoming associated with the **Resurrection of Jesus Christ.**

pomegranate. A pomegranate is a symbol from the ancient myth of Proserpina and her annual return to earth in the spring. Symbolic of the hope of immortality and of **resurrection**, the pomegranate became associated with the **Resurrection of Jesus** and of the
Christians' hope of resurrection. The seeds bursting forth from the pomegranate are also likened to Christ's bursting forth from the tomb on Easter. It may be found in the damasks used for **paraments**, and is frequently used in embroidery.

THE EASTER SEASON

The fifty-day season from Easter to Pentecost Sunday. The liturgical color throughout the Easter season is white.

The Octave of Easter. The eight days from Easter Sunday to the first Sunday following Easter.

The Sundays of Easter. Each of the Sundays in the Easter season traditionally has a different name.

- **Quasimodo Geniti.** The Sunday after Easter (Easter 2). Also known as *Low Sunday*. Named from the first words of the **introit** in Latin: *Quasi modo geniti*, "Like newborn babies" (1 Pet. 2:2).
- **Misericordias Domini.** The third Sunday of Easter. The name is derived from the first words of the **introit** in Latin: *Misericordia Domini plena est terra*, "Of the mercy of the Lord the earth is full."
- **Jubilate.** (Latin, "rejoice.") The fourth Sunday of Easter. Its name is taken from the first Latin word of the **introit**: *Jubilate Deo, omnis terra, alleluia*, "Shout with joy to God, all the earth, alleluia" (Ps. 66:1.)
- **Cantate.** (Latin, "sing.") The fifth Sunday of Easter. The name is taken from the first word of the **introit** in Latin: *Cantate Domino canticum novum, alleluia*, "Sing to the LORD a

new song, alleluia" (Ps. 98:1). This Sunday is also known as *Good Shepherd Sunday*, after the Gospel reading from John 10.

- **Rogate.** (Latin, "ask.") The Sunday before Ascension and the sixth of Easter. The name is taken from the Gospel reading from John 14.

Rogation Days. The Monday, Tuesday, and Wednesday before **Ascension Day**, when God's blessing is asked, particularly for a successful harvest.

ASCENSION DAY

The Thursday forty days after Easter, on which the Ascension of our Lord is commemorated (Acts 1:1–11). (The old English popular name for Ascension is "Holy Thursday," but today this name is restricted to the Thursday in Holy Week, also called **Maundy Thursday**).

Exaudi. The name of the Sunday after Ascension Day, taken from the first word of the **introit** in Latin: *Exaudi Domine, vocem meam*, "Hear my voice with which I have cried to thee, O Lord."

PENTECOST

(Greek, "fiftieth.") Also called *Whitsunday*, Pentecost is the fiftieth day after Easter, the eighth Sunday of the Easter season. It is observed in commemoration of the descent of the Holy Spirit upon the disciples in the form of cloven tongues of fire. Peter was the preacher on that day, and three thousand were baptized (Acts 2:1–41). The name Whitsunday comes from the custom of robing those to be confirmed in white vestments. Liturgical color: red.

ORDINARY TIME 2

(Also known as the *Season after Pentecost* or the *Trinity Season*.) A continuation of Ordinary Time 1, this period forms the longest period of the church year, lasting twenty-two to twenty-seven Sundays, depending on the date of Easter. This is the second half of the church year, and the emphasis during this period is the Christian life. It is followed by **Advent**, which marks the beginning of the church year. Liturgical color: green.

Trinity Sunday. The first Sunday after Pentecost, celebrating the **Holy Trinity**. Liturgical color: white.

The Body and Blood of Christ or **Corpus Christi.** A celebration of the institution and the gift of the **Eucharist**, first observed in the thirteenth century. In the universal calendar of the Roman Catholic Church, Corpus Christi is observed the Thursday after Trinity Sunday; in the United States and Canada, it is observed the Sunday after Trinity Sunday. Liturgical color: red.

Sacred Heart of Jesus [movable]
(Roman calendar only; observed on the Friday following Trinity Sunday.) A solemnity unique to the Roman calendar dating from the thirteenth century. The Sacred Heart of Jesus is a devotion to Christ that venerates both the physical and divine heart of Jesus as symbolic of his redemptive love.

Immaculate Heart of Mary [movable]
(Roman calendar only; observed on the Saturday following Trinity Sunday.) An optional memorial of the Virgin Mary, promoted from the seventeenth century, that grew out of the practice of devotion to the Sacred Heart of Jesus.

Feast of Christ the King. Added to the calendar in the early part of the twentieth century, this day honors Jesus Christ in all his power and authority, affirming in particular his messianic kingship. Observed on the last Sunday of the church year, it is followed by **Advent**. Liturgical color: white or gold.

THE SANCTORAL CYCLE

Sometimes called the *Sanctorale* or the *Proper of Saints*. This calendar includes holy days and saints' days. **Holy days** are days dedicated to remembering important events connected with the life of Jesus Christ or persons linked to him. **Saints' days** are dates in the church year commemorating the birth or death of the **Apostles** and other saints.

In the Roman Church, the calendar of saints is very large and diverse, dependent on a complex tradition of canonization. In addition, the Eastern Church has its own distinct calendar of saints who are commemorated. The saints included here are those mentioned in the Bible or have some connection with Jesus Christ and the early Church.

> *The best preparation for prayer is to read the lives of the saints, not from mere curiosity, but quietly and with recollection a little at a time. And to pause whenever you feel your heart touched with devotion.* (St. Philip Neri)[23]

HOW TO RECOGNIZE A SAINT

All saints have their own symbols, something representative of their life and/or death. But common to all saints, of course, is the **halo** or **nimbus** (Latin, "cloud"), which is a zone of light behind the head of a sacred or divine personage in a painting or a piece of statuary to denote their great dignity. Carried over from Greek and Roman representations of gods and civil rulers, the nimbus usually takes the shape of a circle, square, or triangle in Christian art. The **Virgin**

Mary is portrayed with circular nimbus, often decorated with a ring of stars around her head. Saints and **martyrs** have a disk-shaped nimbus. For God the Father, it is triangular, and for God the Son, it may be a ring. In portrayals of God the Father, of Christ, and of the **Holy Spirit**, the **Trinity** is often symbolized by three rays. For those still living, the nimbus is square or oblong.

WHO ARE THE SAINTS?

apostle. (Greek, "messenger.") The term denoting the Twelve whom Jesus trained as his disciples and sent forth to spread the gospel. Although not among the Twelve, Paul and Barnabas are also numbered among the Apostles. The symbols of an apostle include the miter and staff, representative of their roles as bishops of the church. The Apostles are listed in Matthew 10:2–4; Mark 3:16–19; Luke 6:14–16; Acts 1:13, and though the order of the names varies, Peter is always first and Judas Iscariot last.

doctor of the Church. A theologian whose teachings have influenced the whole Christian church. A rare title, offered only posthumously to one who has been canonized or beatified. The Four Doctors of the Greek Church are St. Basil the Great, St. Gregory Nazianzen, St. John Chrysostom, and St. Athanasius; Four Great Doctors of the Latin Church are St. Ambrose, St. Jerome, St. Augustine, and St. Gregory the Great.

evangelist. (From *evangel*, Greek, "Good news.") The writers of the "good news" of the Gospels: Matthew, Mark, Luke, and John. The symbols of the four Evangelists are a winged man (Matthew), a winged lion (Mark), a winged ox (Luke), and an eagle (John), images found in Ezekiel 1:10 and Revelation 4:7. These symbols are shown in different configurations, such as the **quatrefoil**, a conventionalized flower with four petals, each bearing the symbol of one of the evangelists.

Other symbols include:
- **dove**, on shoulder of Evangelist or Apostle symbolizes divine inspiration.
- **pen** or **pen and inkwell** represents divine authorship.
- **scroll** or **book** represents divine authorship.

martyr. (Greek, "witness.") One who loses his or her life for the faith. Stephen, who was stoned to death for his faith in Jesus as the Christ, was the first Christian martyr (*Protomartyr*).

SYMBOLS OF MARTYRDOM

blood. Symbolic of blood shed in defense of the Gospel.

crown. When worn by a martyr, it signifies victory over sin and death, a sign of honor and victory. In some cases, it indicates that the martyr was of royal blood. When held by a martyr, it signifies a virgin martyr. A *wreath* is a form of crown.

> *Blessed is the man who perseveres under trial, because when he has stood the test, he will receive the crown of life that God has promised to those who love him. (James 1:12)*

palm. In the pre-Christian world, the palm signified victory over the enemy and was used in funerary decoration. It was a symbol that carried over into the early Church, becoming a symbol of spiritual victory, victory over sin and death, especially death through martyrdom.

> *After this I looked and there before me was a great multitude that no one could count, from every nation, tribe, people and language, standing before the throne and in front of the Lamb. They were wearing white robes and were holding palm branches in their hands. And they cried out in a loud voice:*

"Salvation belongs to our God, who sits on the throne, and to the Lamb." (Rev. 7:9–10)

red rose. Symbolizes blood, and speaks of martyrdom. (Roses also appear in white or yellow. The white rose represents purity and the yellow rose unattainable perfection or papal favor.)

stag, hunted. Symbolizes the persecution of early Christians.

INSTRUMENTS OF MARTYRDOM

Some instruments of martyrdom that may appear in art or other depictions of saints:

anvil. Used to cut off limbs. St. Adrian.

arrows. May indicate either dedication to the service of God as a spiritual warrior or else the instrument of martyrdom. St. Ursula, St. Sebastian.

battle-axe, axe. Often, death by beheading. St. Matthew. With two stones: St. Matthias. With oar and saw, or two oars: St. Simon. Sometimes also St. Jude.

cauldron. Filled with boiling oil. St. John the Apostle, St. Boniface, etc.

cross. Death by crucifixion. Cross may be shown in different positions, to indicate the position of the cross on which the particular martyr died. St. Andrew, St. Peter.

fire. Death by fire. May be shown with a stake, as St. Agatha and others. May also be shown with burning coals or blazing wood.

fuller's club, bat. A tool used by fabric makers in a process called fulling, in which the cloth was beaten with clubs or bats. Death by beating. St. James the Less, St. Simon, St. Jude.

gridiron. Martyrdom by roasting over a fire. St. Lawrence.

grindstone, millstone. Death or torture by being crushed or by drowning.

halberd. A weapon that consisted of an axe blade topped by a lance-like spike mounted on a long shaft. On the opposite side of the axe blade was a hook for engaging enemies on horseback. This weapon allowed for hacking and for piercing. (See also lance.)

head. Many saints who were beheaded are represented in Christian art as carrying their severed heads.

knife. Death by stabbing or flaying. St. Bartholomew, St. James the Less.

knotted club. Death or torture by beating. St. Jude, St. Philip.

lance or halberd. Death by impaling. St. Jude, St. Thomas.

poniard. A small dagger with a slim triangular or square blade. St. Lucia.

saw. Death by being sawn asunder. St. Simon Zelotes.

skin. Human skin: Death by flaying. St. Bartholomew.

sword. Martyr's death by sword, especially if shown with a palm. Otherwise may simply signify the attribute of a warrior saint.

---

wheel, set with knives. According to legend, St. Catherine was ordered by the Emperor Maximinus II (or Maxentius) to be bound between four wheels rimmed with knives to be hacked to death.

OTHER SYMBOLS OR ATTRIBUTES OF SAINTS

arm. Strength, protection, defense.

armor. Warrior saint. Christian faith as the protection from evil. Also may represent the armor of God: Belt or Girdle of Truth, Breastplate of Righteousness, Shield of Faith, Helmet of Salvation, Sword of the Spirit (Eph. 6:13–17).

aspergillum (Sometimes called *asperges*, from the opening words of the **Sprinkling Rite**, Latin.) Represents holiness, purity.

balances (scales). Justice or judgment. May be shown with a sword. Often carried by **St. Michael**.

basket. Charity to the poor.

beehive. Great eloquence. St. Bernard of Clairvaux, St. Ambrose.

book or scroll. Authorship, writings, or wisdom. By extension, represents a person known for his learning or for his writing. If a writer, sometimes accompanied by a pen and inkwell (inkhorn). If a book is open, it denotes wisdom (Isa. 29:11–12). If closed, a book may denote mystery; or in representations of the Virgin Mary, it denotes her virginity.

book, font, and chalice. The means of Grace.

bow. War, worldly power (Jer. 49:35).

bread. The Bread of Life, Jesus Christ (see **the seven I ams**). Also denotes charity to the poor.

bridle. Self-control, temperance.

cable, rope, or **chain.** Strength.

candle, lighted. Represents an individual human life. Also may be shown being held by St. Joseph of Nazareth to represent the birth of Jesus, the light of the world.

casket or **small box.** Relic of a saint.

chains, broken. Liberation of the imprisoned. Symbolically, sin overcome.

child, naked. The human soul. A naked child rising out of the mouth of a dying person: the release of the soul. A naked child in scales or balances: the weighing of souls.

church building. Founder of a church.

church model, held in the hands of a saint. Signifies a person who served to build up the Christian Church; also great builders of cathedrals, abbeys, priories, churches, and the like.

cross or **crucifix.** A person of great holiness.

crown or **other emblem of royalty.** Indicates royalty or victory over sin and death. A wreath may represent a crown as well.

dove. On shoulder of an **evangelist** or **apostle**: divine inspiration. On shoulder of any saint: enlightenment.

earthen vessels. Humanity, mortality (Isa. 64:8).

fan (winnowing fan or fork). Purification (Matt. 3:12).

flag or **banner.** Military service.

fountain. Salvation (Zech. 13:1).

halo or **nimbus.** A holy life.

hand, extended: protection. Hand, palm upward: invitation.

handcuffs, broken. The symbol of a saint devoted to serving the imprisoned.

harp. Music, divine worship, joy (Rev. 5:8).

heart. Christian charity. A heart with a flame: intense zeal or devotion. A heart with cross and anchor: Faith, Hope, and Charity.

horn (animal). Ancient symbol of strength and power, especially from God.

lamb. A sinful, lost, and needy human in need of the **Good Shepherd** (Luke 15:1–7; John 10:1–18).

lamp. Wisdom, especially wisdom from God (Ps. 119:105).

lamp and book. Enlightenment, knowledge.

lily and rose. Virgin martyr.

lion. Hermit saint.

lyre. Music.

miter or **pastoral staff.** Bishop, abbot, abbess.

money. An open bag: charity to the poor. Coins at the feet of a saint: the renunciation of worldly gain; also charity to the poor.

padlock. Secrecy, discretion.

pen. Authorship. With inkwell (inkhorn): an **evangelist** or a **doctor of the Church.**

purse, open. Charity to the poor.

ring. Symbol of eternity and an unbreakable union, as in marriage. A **nun**'s ring represents her spiritual marriage to Christ. A ring also symbolizes authority, especially a **bishop**'s ring.

rock. Stability, firmness. May symbolize Jesus Christ, the Rock of Salvation; the **Church**; or **St. Peter.**

ruins. Of cities or buildings, shown in classical architecture, represents the decay of the world, especially the pagan world.

scepter. Symbol of authority, especially earthly authority.

scroll or **book**. Authorship, writings, or wisdom. By extension, represents a person known for his learning or for his writing. If a writer, sometimes accompanied by a pen and inkwell (inkhorn).

scroll, with music on it. St. Ambrose, St. Gregory the Great, St. Cecilia.

shoes or **sandals.** Standing empty near a barefoot person, indicates that the person is standing on holy ground, just as Moses was commanded to remove his shoes because he was standing on holy ground (Ex. 3:1–6).

staff. A pilgrim or hermit.

sword. A symbol of martyrdom; also warfare. A blunt sword represents mercy; a pointed sword or sword with balances symbolizes justice; a sword held with two hands represents the civil authority; a sword held with the hilt upward speaks of consecration and allegiance.

tower. Symbolizes defense, strength, especially from God.

triple tiara or **crown.** A pope.

veil. The renunciation of the world; also modesty and chastity, or mystery.

weather vane. Spiritual instability.

wheel, potter's. Recalls that human lives are shaped by divine power (Isa. 45:9, 64:8; Jer. 18:6–10).

wolf, bear, or other **wild beast.** Symbolizes a person who successfully ministered to the pagans.

THE VIRGIN MARY

To you we flee for shelter and compassion, mother of God.
You alone are chaste and blessed; do not disregard our prayers
in this hour of need, but deliver us from danger.
(Early Christian Prayer)[24]

Mary is honored by all Christians as the mother of Jesus, the one through whom the promised Redeemer came. Considered preeminent among all saints, Mary is venerated in both the Eastern Church and the Roman Church as the merciful mother, the personification of purity and grace. Devotion to the Virgin Mary has comprised a large part of the piety in these traditions from the time of the early Church through the present. Mary is an intercessor, a protector, and an advocate, and is compassionate and merciful. She is also called: *Blessed Virgin Mary* (BVM), *Queen of Heaven, Theotokos* (Greek, "God-bearer"), *Mother of God, Madonna.* Liturgical color: white.

The **solemnities of Mary** include:
- The Feast of the Immaculate Conception, December 8;
- Mary, Mother of God, January 1;
- the Annunciation of the Lord, March 25;
- the Assumption of the Blessed Virgin Mary, August 15.

The **feasts of Mary** are:
- The Presentation of Our Lord, February 2;
- the Visitation of the Blessed Virgin Mary, May 31;
- the Birth of the Blessed Virgin Mary, September 8.

SYMBOLS OF THE VIRGIN MARY

In art, Mary is identifiable by the particular shade of blue of her mantle. Blue represents heaven and heavenly love, and it has become the color associated with Mary as Queen of Heaven.

apple. Mary is sometimes shown holding a apple, signifying her role as the second Eve; as sin entered the world through Eve, so redemption entered the world through Mary.

book. Sealed: refers to Mary's chastity.

crown, especially a crown tipped with twelve stars. From Revelation 12:1. Symbolic of Mary as the Queen of Heaven. Sometimes shown as a crown of stars and lilies.

dove. In pictures of the Annunciation, a dove often hovers over the Virgin Mary, representing the Holy Spirit.

ear. In old German art, the Conception of our Lord was often pictured as a tiny child flying into the ear of the Virgin, signifying the Annunciation.

earth (orb) under the feet of the Virgin. Refers to Mary's role in fulfilling God's curse over sin in Genesis 3:15.

fleur-de-lis. The fleur-de-lis is a stylized representation of the lily, and was adopted as a symbol of royalty in France. As such, it is symbolic of the Virgin Mary, Queen of Heaven.

gate, closed. Refers to Mary's unblemished virginity.

heart, pierced with a sword and shown sometimes with wings. Refers to Simeon's words recorded in Luke 2:34–35:
Then Simeon blessed them and said to Mary, his mother:
"This child is destined to cause the falling and rising of many

*in Israel, and to be a sign that will be spoken against, so that
the thoughts of many hearts will be revealed. And a sword
will pierce your own soul too."*

iris. Sometimes known as the *sword lily*, taken as an allusion to
Mary's suffering at the passion of Christ. Shown particularly in
representations of the **Immaculate Conception**.

 lily. *lilium candidum* (Latin) or **Madonna lily**. Purity;
innocence; virginity. Appears especially in depictions of the **Annunciation**, with St. Gabriel carrying
a lily or with one shown growing at the Virgin's side.

moon, crescent. In depictions of the **Immaculate Conception**,
Mary is often shown standing on a crescent moon. Combines
both Old Testament (Song 6:10) and New Testament (Rev. 12:1)
references, showing Mary's beauty and her reflection of the glory
of Jesus Christ as the moon reflects the light of the sun. See also
sun and moon, below.

palm. Mary's triumph over sin and death.

rose. White and without thorns, indicating the purity of Mary,
who was free of the sins (thorns) of the Fall.

scepter. Sometimes shown tipped with fleur-de-lis. Symbolic of
Mary's role as the Queen of Heaven.

serpent, bruised. Under the foot of Mary. Refers to Mary's role in
fulfilling God's curse over sin in Genesis 3:15.

star. A single star speaks to Mary's perpetual virginity—as a star
shines without losing its brightness or power, so Mary bore Jesus
without losing her chastity.

stars, circle of twelve. Used in depictions of the **Immaculate Conception** and of Mary as Queen of Heaven (Rev. 12:1).

sun and moon at Mary's feet. From Rev. 12:1. Symbolic of Mary's role as the Queen of Heaven.

OTHER FAMILIAR TITLES OF MARY

Derived from *Song of Solomon:*
- **sealed fountain** or **sealed spring.** From Song of Solomon 4:12. Refers to Mary's virginity
- **fountain of living waters.** From Song of Solomon 4:15.
- **enclosed garden.** From Song of Solomon 4:12. Refers to Mary's virginity.

Derived from the *Litany of Loreto* (1587), **sometimes called the Litany of the Blessed Virgin Mary:**
- **mirror.** Called "Mirror of Justice" (*Speculum justitiae*) in the Litany of Loreto. Sometimes called *speculum* (Latin). Refers to the passage from the Wisdom of Solomon 7:26: "For she is a reflection of eternal light, a spotless mirror of the working of God, and an image of his goodness" (NRSV).
- **Seat of wisdom** (*Sedes sapientiae*). Wisdom became incarnate through Mary's womb.
- **Vessel: spiritual vessel** (*Vas spirituale*); **vessel of honor** (*Vas honorabile*); **singular vessel of devotion** (*Vas insigne devotionis*). Mary was the vessel that carried God into the world.
- **Mystical rose** (*Rosa mystica*). See rose, above.
- **Tower of David** (*Turris davidica*). From Song of Solomon 4:4. Mary is the glory of the House of David.

- **Tower of ivory** (*Turris eburnea*). From Song of Solomon 7:4. Ivory speaks of peace and wealth. Mary reaches to the heavens as a sign of peace and blessing.
- **House of gold** (*Domus aurea*). Solomon's Temple, the house of God, was covered in gold, and so Mary, whose womb housed the Lord, was a temple, a House of Gold.
- **Ark of the Covenant** (*Foederis arca*). The Ark was the location of God's Presence in Israel and held the tablets of the Law; in the Incarnation, Mary's womb held the maker of the Law and made God present to humanity.
- **Gate of heaven** (*Janua coeli*). Mary was the gate by which Christ came to the world.
- **Morning Star** (*Stella matutina*). As the Planet Venus— the morning star—precedes the coming of the sun and morning, so Mary heralds the coming of Jesus and his redemption.

Monograms of Mary

- **M.** Abbreviation for *Ave Maria*, Gabriel's opening words to Mary at the Annunciation.
- **M**, or **MR**, *Maria Regina* (Latin). With or without a crown above. Mary, Queen of Heaven.
- **MA DI**, *Mater Dei* (Latin). "Mother of God."

The Seven Joys and the Seven Sorrows of Mary

- **Seven Joys of the Virgin Mary.** The Annunciation, Visitation, Nativity, Epiphany, Presentation, Finding her Son in the Temple, the Assumption.
- **Seven Sorrows of the Virgin**. The Prophecy of Simeon, the Flight into Egypt, the Loss of Her Son at Twelve, the Betrayal, the Crucifixion, the Entombment, the Ascension.

APOSTLES, SYMBOLS OF — Among others, the most commonly used are:

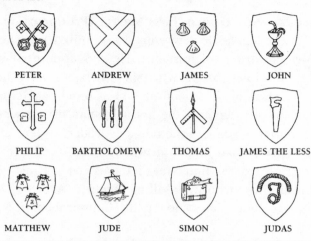

PETER	ANDREW	JAMES	JOHN
PHILIP	BARTHOLOMEW	THOMAS	JAMES THE LESS
MATTHEW	JUDE	SIMON	JUDAS

THE SANCTORAL CYCLE

November 30—Saint Andrew, Apostle

The first disciple called by Jesus, Andrew left his fishing nets and spent the rest of his life bringing others to Christ, beginning with his brother Simon Peter (John 1:35–42; see also Matt. 4:18–20; Mark 1:16–18). According to tradition, Andrew preached in many countries, including Scotland, Russia, and finally, Greece, where he was martyred by crucifixion. His symbol is a **saltire** (or X-shaped) **cross**, signifying his crucifixion. The cross may be shown alone or with other symbols that reflect his life as a fisherman and his call to become a fisher of men (Mark 1:16–18): a fishing net, a fishing hook, a boat hook, fish. Liturgical color: red.

December 8—The Feast of the Immaculate Conception

A solemnity of Mary (Roman calendar only). This celebration of the conception of Mary, who was said to have been free from sin from the moment of her conception, is observed nine months before the celebration of her birth on September 8. It became a feast in the seventh century.

December 21—Saint Thomas, Apostle. See July 3.

December 26—St. Stephen, First Martyr (Protomartyr)

A Hellenistic Jew who was a gifted preacher and performer of miracles. He was appointed by the disciples, along with six others, to carry out the work of a deacon in the Church at Jerusalem. Stephen became the first Christian martyr when his preaching outraged some of the religious leaders in Jerusalem so much that they stoned him to death (Acts 6:8–7:60). It was at Stephen's death that we find Saul of Tarsus (later, Paul) holding the clothes of those who were killing Stephen (Acts 8:1; 22:20). His symbols include stones and a palm. Liturgical color: red.

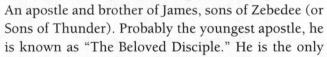

December 27—Saint John, Apostle, Evangelist

An apostle and brother of James, sons of Zebedee (or Sons of Thunder). Probably the youngest apostle, he is known as "The Beloved Disciple." He is the only one of the Twelve to have died a natural death. The Gospel of John; three Epistles: First, Second, and Third John; and Revelation are ascribed to him. His symbol as an evangelist is the eagle, which is often incorporated in the structure of the lectern because its outstretched wings represent the spread of the Gospel. As an apostle, he is also shown with a serpent and a chalice (death by poisoning) or cauldron of oil (death by boiling), representing the attempts on his life. He is also sometimes shown with a scroll inscribed with the words *Sc. Joannes* or *Sc. Johannes*, indicating his authorship. Liturgical color: white.

December 28—Feast of The Holy Innocents
A feast commemorating Herod's slaughter of the children under two years of age at Bethlehem (Matt. 2:16). Liturgical color: red.

January 1
The Octave of Christmas
Mary, Mother of God (Roman calendar)
The Holy Name of Our Lord Jesus Christ
(Anglican and **Protestant** calendars)
The Feast of the Circumcision (old designation)
A solemnity of Mary commemorating the circumcision of the infant Jesus (Luke 2:21), when Jesus was given his name (according to Jewish custom). Liturgical color: white.

January 18—The Confession of Saint Peter, Apostle
(Anglican and **Protestant** calendars, new to the 1979 Episcopal **The Book of Common Prayer**.) Commemorates Peter's response to Jesus' question, "Who do you say I am?" "You are the Christ, the Son of the living God" (Matt. 16:15–16). His symbol is crossed gold and silver keys, which represent Peter's authority to bind and to loose that was given to him by Jesus in response to his confession: "Blessed are you, Simon son of Jonah, for this was not revealed to you by man, but by my Father in heaven. And I tell you that you are Peter, and on this rock I will build my church, and the gates of Hades will not overcome it. I will give you the keys of the kingdom of heaven; whatever you bind on earth will be bound in heaven, and whatever you loose on earth will be loosed in heaven" (Matt. 16:17–19). The inverted cross and keys may appear together or with other symbols such as a **patriarchal cross** (first bishop of Rome), **scroll** or **book** (authorship), or **chains** or **fetters** (imprisonment), and rock (as above). Liturgical color: red.

January 25—The Conversion of Saint Paul, Apostle

Paul's first encounter with Christians was as a vicious persecutor, but this changed while he was on his way to Damascus to root out the Christians. Paul was confronted by a light from heaven and a voice that asked, "Saul,

Saul, why do you persecute me?" The result was his **conversion** (Acts 9:1–22). Paul became the apostle who took the gospel to the Gentiles and is said to have authored at least thirteen of the twenty-one epistles of the New Testament, expanding the influence and defining the faith of the Christian Church. His death is commemorated with that of St. Peter, on **June 29**. The symbols of Paul feature a book (or scroll), recalling his authorship of twelve epistles; and a sword, cross-hilted, referring to his death by beheading, a right that he claimed as a Roman citizen. Sometimes the book reads *Spiritus Gladius,* (Latin) "Sword of the Spirit" (Eph. 6:17). Other symbols include:

- *a serpent*, shown sometimes with fire (from Acts 28:1–6);
- three *fountains* (in heraldic images) from the legend that when he was beheaded, three fountains sprang up at the place his head fell to the ground;
- *Shield of Faith*, a rayed Latin cross on a shield, from Eph. 6:16;
- *a phoenix*, for his teaching on the Resurrection; and
- *a scourge*, for his repeated persecution.

Liturgical color: red.

February 2—Presentation of Our Lord
A feast commemorating the presentation of the Infant Jesus at the Temple by Mary and Joseph (Luke 2:22–40) forty days after his birth. It was during this visit to the Temple that Jesus was received by the aged Anna and by Simeon, who uttered his beloved thanksgiving to God (sometimes called the *Canticle of Simeon* or **Nunc Dimittis**). This feast may also be called *Candlemas*, as candles are lighted in remembrance of Simeon's words, "A Light to lighten the Gentiles." Liturgical color: white.

- **Feast of the Purification.** Part of the Feast of Presentation. It recalls a special sacrifice that a mother brought to the temple upon the birth of a son, according to the Old Testament Laws (Exod. 13:12–13; Lev. 12:2–8).

- **Churching of Women.** An ancient ceremony for the purpose of readmitting a woman to the church forty days after childbirth. It corresponds to the Feast of Purification of Mary, and the Presentation of Christ, or Candlemas.

February 22—The Chair of Saint Peter, Apostle
(Roman calendar only)
Recalling the chair or seat (Latin, *cathedra*) from which a **bishop** presides and preaches, this day commemorates the role of Saint Peter as the Bishop of Rome and pastor of the whole Church. Peter was the author of two pastoral epistles that bear his name. See also **January 18, the Confession of Saint Peter**, and **June 29, Saint Peter and Saint Paul.**

March 19—Saint Joseph,
Husband of the Blessed Virgin Mary
Joseph is honored for his spiritual acuity and his faithful care of Mary and Jesus. He is mentioned in the genealogies of Matthew and Luke as well as in their infancy narratives (Matthew 1–2, Luke 1–2), but Joseph is not mentioned again after the family's visit to the Temple when Jesus was twelve years old. He is also remembered on May 1, as Saint Joseph the Worker, in keeping with his role as a provider for his family. His symbols include a carpenter's plane, saw, and hatchet (representative of his trade) and a lily (for purity). He may also be shown with a budding or flowering staff, from a legend. Liturgical color: white.

March 25—The Annunciation of
Our Lord Jesus Christ to the Blessed
Virgin Mary or The Annunciation of the Lord
A solemnity of Mary that commemorates the visitation of the angel Gabriel to Mary to announce the conception of our Lord (Luke 1:26–38). Liturgical color: white.

April 25—Saint Mark, Evangelist

John Mark was one of the four companions of Peter and Paul on their missionary journeys. According to tradition, he was the boy who escaped capture when Jesus was arrested (Mark 14:51). He founded the Christian church in Alexandria, Egypt, and was martyred there. He is the author of "The Gospel According to Saint Mark" in which he presents Christ as the King. His symbol as an evangelist is a winged lion with a **nimbus** in accordance with his presentation of the royal character of Christ. In celebration of his role as the author of a Gospel he is sometimes shown with a scroll inscribed with the words *Pax Tibi* (Latin, "Peace to you"). Liturgical color: red.

May 3—Saint Philip and Saint James, Apostles

(On May 1 in Anglican and **Protestant** calendars.)

Both are lesser figures among the disciples. Nothing is known about Philip save what was recorded in the Gospel stories and in the listings of the Twelve. We first see Philip when he is called by Jesus and in turn introduces Nathanael to him (John 1:43–46; see also John 6:1–14; 12:20–22; 14:8–11). Philip the Apostle is not to be confused with Philip the **deacon** who was appointed with Stephen (Acts 6:5), evangelized Samaria (Acts 8:5–13), and appeared to the Ethiopian eunuch (Acts 8:26–40).

James the Less (or Younger, or Minor) is identified as the son of Alphaeus in the listings of the Apostles. In the Roman church, he is considered to be the James who was numbered among the "brothers" of Jesus, and was later the **bishop** of the church at Jerusalem and the author of the epistle that bears his name. In the Anglican and **Protestant** traditions, however, James the Less is distinct from James, the brother of Jesus. (See October 23, **Saint James of Jerusalem, Brother of Our Lord Jesus Christ, and Martyr**). Also, this James is not to be confused with **James the Greater**, brother of John (see July 25).

The symbols of Philip are a **Latin cross** with a loaf of bread on either side under the cross arm, indicating the manner of his death and his remark at the feeding of the five thousand (John 6:7). Sometimes he is represented by a **tau cross** and a basket, or by an inverted **Latin cross** or a red **saltire cross**.

The symbols of James the Less are multiple. His primary symbol is a saw to indicate that according to tradition he was dismembered. Other traditions indicate that before he was dismembered, he was thrown off of a wall of the Temple in Jerusalem, then stoned. When he hadn't died, he was finally clubbed to death with a **fuller's bat**, and finally his body was dismembered with a saw. Liturgical color: red.

May 14—Saint Matthias the Apostle

(On February 24 in Anglican and **Protestant** calendars.) Matthias is mentioned in the New Testament only at the time of his selection (Acts 1:21–26). One tradition states he preached in Judea and was stoned, then beheaded. Another tradition says he preached in Jerusalem then went to Colchis (a region on the eastern edge of the Black Sea, in today's Georgia) where he died by crucifixion. He is believed to have been martyred in AD 64, the same year as Saint Mark. One of his symbols is a pair of dice, because the lot fell on him to take the place of Judas among the Twelve. Other symbols include a **lance** with three stones; an open **book** with **battle-axe**, large knife, or **halberd**; or a sword held by the point. Liturgical color: red

May 31—The Visitation of the Blessed Virgin Mary

A solemnity of Mary, celebrating the visit of Mary to her relative Elizabeth, the mother of John the Baptist (Luke 1:39-56), following the Annunciation. When Elizabeth heard Mary's greeting, Elizabeth's child John leapt in her womb and she blessed Mary for her faith. Mary responded with her hymn of praise to God, the *Magnificat*. Liturgical color: white.

The Ascension (Thursday before the Seventh Sunday of Easter). Technically part of the **Sanctoral Cycle, Ascension Day** is included in the **Easter season** section (above).

June 24—The Nativity of Saint John the Baptist The life of John the Baptist was intertwined with the life of Jesus from birth (Luke 1). As an adult, John lived in the desert and preached **repentance** in preparation for the coming of the **Messiah**, thereby serving as the herald for Jesus. Ultimately, he was beheaded by Herod Antipas (Matt. 14:3–12; Mark 6:17–29), an event that is memorialized on **August 29**. The symbols of John the Baptist include:

- **rough, camel's-hair coat**
- **charger** or **platter**, with a **severed head**
- **lamb, holding a banner of victory** (a three-pointed white pennant, charged with a red Latin cross)
- **leather girdle**
- **locust, with or without a leather girdle**
- **scroll** or **book, with *Ecce Agnus Dei*** (Latin), "Behold the Lamb of God" (John 1:35–36)
- **scroll** or **book**, with ***Vox clamantis in deserto*** (Latin), "the voice (of one) crying in the wilderness" (Isa. 40:3–5; Luke 3:4–6)

Liturgical color: red

June 29—Saint Peter and Saint Paul, Apostles
According to legend, Peter was crucified on the same day that Paul was beheaded in Rome under the persecutions of Nero. Their deaths are therefore commemorated together in this important solemnity, which also acknowledges the Church in Rome. (**The Confession of Saint Peter** is commemorated on January 18, the **Chair of Saint Peter** on February 22, and the **Conversion of Saint Paul** on January 25.) Liturgical color: red.

July 3—Saint Thomas, Apostle

(On December 21 in Anglican and **Protestant** calendars.)

A disciple of Christ's who was also called Didymus (Greek, "twin"). Thomas was always the realist, albeit a courageous realist (see John 11:16; 14:5), to the point of being labeled "doubting" Thomas (John 20:24–29). According to tradition, Thomas was a **missionary** in the East, particularly to Parthia (modern-day Iran) and India, where he was martyred. His symbols are most commonly a spear or lance (the instrument of his death) behind a builder's square (representative of his life as the builder of a great palace in India, and by extention, a builder of the church). Symbols may also include a girdle or belt from a second occasion of doubting: When Thomas doubted the **Assumption** of Mary, she lowered her belt or girdle down from heaven to convince him.

July 22—Saint Mary Magdalene

A memorial commemorating one of the Lord's most faithful disciples who had richly received his grace. Jesus had cast seven demons out of Mary (Luke 8:1–2), and she became one of the women who traveled with Jesus and the Twelve. She was present at the Crucifixion (Matt. 27:56) and among the women at the tomb on Easter morning (Matt. 28:1). Mary is also the first person to whom Jesus first revealed himself after his **Resurrection** (Matt. 28:9–10; John 20:11–18). Because she ran to tell the disciples about the Resurrection, she is sometimes called "the apostle to the apostles." In the Roman church, she is considered the same person as Mary of Bethany, sister to Martha and Lazarus. In the Eastern church, and for Anglicans and Lutherans, Mary Magdalene and Mary of Bethany are two separate women. The symbols of Mary Magdalene include a jar or box (casket) of ointment, for the spices she was taking to the grave of Jesus (Luke 24:1), or alternatively (if regarded as the same woman) as the jar of ointment she broke over the feet of Jesus (John 12:3). (See also July 29, **Mary of Bethany**.) Liturgical color: white.

July 25—Saint James, Apostle
(James the Greater, James the Elder, James Major)

An apostle and brother of John, with whom he fished and fought. They were given the title "Sons of Thunder" (Mark 3:17). The first of the disciples to be martyred and the only one whose death is recorded in the New Testament (Acts 12:2). With Peter and John, he was one of the inner circle of disciples closest to Jesus. His symbol is three scallop shells, representing the missionary journeys he made to establish the Christian faith in Spain. Often the scallop shell is shown with other symbols of pilgrimage: a pilgrim's staff, a wallet, a pilgrim's hat, and the letters *St. J.* His symbols are also accompanied by a sword, symbolic of the means of his martyrdom. Liturgical color: red.

July 29—Saint Martha of Bethany and Saint Mary of Bethany

Martha and Mary were friends of Jesus who with their brother Lazarus regularly hosted Jesus in their home in Bethany. They are most remembered for the visit when Martha insisted that Jesus make Mary help with their hostessing responsibilities (Luke 10:38–42). Both Mary and Martha were utterly committed to Jesus. When Lazarus died, and Jesus arrived too late to save him, Martha went out to meet him. Despite her grief, she confidently declared her faith: "I believe that you are the Christ, the Son of God, who was to come into the world" (John 11:20–27). Not long after this, after Jesus had raised Lazarus from the dead, Jesus was a guest at their home once again. Mary anointed Jesus' feet with a jar of expensive perfume, and wiped them with her hair (John 12:1–3).

Legend states that once, while preaching, Martha conquered a dragon by sprinkling it with holy water. Her symbols reflect this legend and her role as an efficient household manager and hostess: they include an **aspergillum** (sometimes called *asperges*) and a basin, and sometimes a chatelaine (a ring of keys attached to a belt), a ladle, or another kitchen implement.

Mary is represented by a jar or box of ointment, symbolizing her anointing of Jesus' feet. See also July 22, **Saint Mary Magdalene.** Liturgical color: White.

August 6—The Transfiguration of Our Lord Jesus Christ

From the story in Matthew 17:1–8, Mark 9:2–8, and Luke 9:28–36, when Jesus took Peter, James, and John with him up a high mountain to pray. As he was praying, Jesus was transfigured into a glorified form, and "Two men, Moses and Elijah, appeared in glorious splendor, talking with Jesus" (Luke 9:30–31). In addition to this feast day, the Transfiguration is also celebrated on the last Sunday of the Epiphany season in the Anglican and **Protestant** traditions, and on the second Sunday of Lent in the Roman calendar. Liturgical color: white.

August 15—The Assumption of the Blessed Virgin Mary or Saint Mary the Virgin

(Roman and Anglican calendars.)
A solemnity of Mary that commemorates the dogma that states: "The Immaculate Mother of God, Mary ever Virgin, when the course of her earthly life was finished was taken up body and soul into the glory of heaven." This belief first surfaced in the sixth century and was commemorated on this day, but was not declared dogma until the nineteenth century. Liturgical color: white.

August 24—Saint Bartholomew, Apostle

Bartholomew is one of the Twelve who is mentioned in the lists of disciples (Matt. 10:3; Mark 3:18; Luke 6:14; and Acts 1:13). He is closely associated with Philip and for this reason is sometimes identified as the Nathanael in John's Gospel who is introduced to Jesus by Philip (John 1:45–51). His symbol features three flaying knives, the instruments of his death, or a flaying knife and a book. He is sometimes shown with his skin carried over his arm, or hanging on a cross. Sometimes he is symbolized with a fig or fig tree, recalling his first encounter with Jesus (John 1:47–49). Liturgical color: red.

August 29—Beheading of John the Baptist
(Roman calendar only.) See **June 24, The Nativity of Saint John The Baptist.**

September 8—Birth of the Blessed Virgin Mary or
The Nativity of Mary (Roman and Eastern calendars only.)
This feast of Mary originated in Palestine; the Eastern Churches have celebrated the nativity of Mary on either September 8 or 9 beginning in the earliest times. The feast was carried over into the Western Church in the late seventh century.

September 14—Holy Cross Day or The Triumph of the Cross or Exaltation of the Cross
A feast dating from AD 335 when a church built on the site of the Holy Sepulchre in Jerusalem was dedicated by the Emperor Constantine. Prefigured by Moses' lifting up his staff bearing a serpent, the cross became the means of Christ's victory over death. This feast is celebrated in the Eastern Church and the Western Church alike.

September 21—Saint Matthew, Apostle and Evangelist

 Matthew was a tax collector until Jesus called him to become one of his disciples (Matt. 9:9–13). Identified as Levi in Mark (2:14–17) and Luke (5:27–32), he is the writer of the Gospel that bears his name (the first book of the New Testament). Matthew's symbol as an evangelist is a winged man, because in his Gospel, he emphasizes the humanity of Christ. His symbol as an apostle features three money bags, representing Matthew's days as a tax collector. According to

tradition, Matthew was martyred in Ethiopia by beheading, so he may be symbolized with an **axe** or a **halberd**. Liturgical color: red.

September 29—Saint Michael and All Angels

A feast commemorating Saint Michael, Saint Gabriel, and all other **angels**. Various early Christian writers addressed the order of the celestial hierarchy, until finally Denys the Areopagite established what was considered a definitive list in the fifth century. He wrote that there are nine choirs of celestial beings, ranked in three hierarchies, each containing three choirs, all of whom surround the throne of God to worship him and do his bidding. From highest to lowest, these are: Seraphim, Cherubim, Thrones, Dominations, Virtues, Powers, Principalities, Archangels, and Angels. It is the activities of the last two that are found in Scripture. Liturgical color: white.

- **seraphs** (*seraphim*, Hebrew) are mentioned only once, in Isa. 6:2–3.
- **cherubs** (*cherubim*, Hebrew), though classified with the angels, are more strictly the winged creatures with human-animal form. Described in detail by Ezekiel, then later in Revelation, each "living creature" has four faces, representing the four "excellencies" of the created order: the lion (wild beasts), the ox (domesticated beasts), the eagle (birds), and man (the crown of creation) (Ezek. 9:3; 10:1–22; Rev. 4:6–9; 5:6–14; 6:1–8; 14:3; 15:7; 19:4). The cherubim are the carriers of God, the living chariots, if you will, when God appears to humans (as in 2 Sam. 22:11; Ps. 18:10; Ps. 99:1).

  Cherubim were stationed at the east of Eden with a flaming sword to guard the way to the Tree of Life after Adam and Eve were expelled from the Garden of Eden (Gen. 3:24).

  The holiest places—the places associated with the Presence of God himself—were decorated with images of cherubim. The curtains of the tabernacle were embroidered with images of cherubim (Ex. 26:1). Two cherubim of beaten gold were positioned on the mercy seat above the ark, the place where God would commune with Moses (Ex. 25:18–22; 37:7–9). In the tabernacle and later the temple, God's glory rested between the cherubim (Num. 7:89; 1 Sam. 4:4; 2 Sam. 6:2; 2 Kings 19:15; Ps. 80:1; Ps. 99:1; Isa. 37:16). Solomon's temple featured huge figures of cherubim made specially for this building (1 Kings 6:23–28; 2 Chr. 3:10–13; 5:7–8), as well as carved cherubim decorating its walls (1 Kings 6:29).

The cherubs of Renaissance art—the chubby infants with wings—are works of pure invention.

- **archangel**. A chief angel who acts as a messenger from God to humankind. The archangels Michael and Gabriel are mentioned in the Bible.
- **Michael** (Hebrew, "he who is like unto the Lord") is the one who defeats Satan; his symbol features a sword and scales, for he is said to weigh the souls of men. He may also be shown with a dragon underfoot (Rev. 12:7–9).
- **Gabriel** (Hebrew, "God is Mighty") was the messenger to Zechariah (Luke 1:19) and to Mary at the Annunciation (Luke 1:26). His symbol is a lily or an iris, recalling his role in the Annunciation (Luke 1:26–38). He sometimes is shown with a shield bearing the initials A.M., a reference to Ave Maria, the opening words of the Annunciation. Gabriel may also be shown with a trumpet, as on the Resurrection Day (1 Thess. 4:16).
- Other archangels from apocryphal writings are Raphael (mentioned in Tobit) and Uriel (mentioned in 1 Enoch), who with Michael and Gabriel surround the throne of God.
- **angel**. (Greek, "messenger.") A spiritual being created by God to be his agent and do his will. In Scripture, angels protect, heal, lead, intercede, and execute judgment.
- In art, representations of angels may convey specific meanings:
  angel kneeling: adoration; intercession; thanksgiving.
  angel with hand extended: guardianship.

---

angel with both hands extended: invitation.

angel with trumpet: Resurrection Day.

angel holding chalice: the Agony in Gethsemane.

angel sheathing sword: God's vengeance turned aside.

angel kneeling before an equilateral triangle: adoration.

angel with flaming sword: expulsion from Eden.

October 18—Saint Luke, Evangelist

Not an apostle but an evangelist, Luke is the devoted physician who traveled with Paul. He had studied at Antioch and probably was converted after Christ's ascension. He is the author of the Gospel that bears his name and "The Acts of the Apostles." His symbol is the winged ox (the sacrificial animal), symbolic of the atoning sacrifice of Jesus that is emphasized in his Gospel. Liturgical Color: red.

October 23—Saint James of Jerusalem,
Brother of Our Lord Jesus Christ, and Martyr

(In Anglican and **Protestant** calendars.)

This day honors the man identified as a brother of Jesus (Matt. 13:55; Mark 6:3), who publicly challenged him and misunderstood his mission (John 7:2–5). But after his **Resurrection**, Jesus appeared to James (1 Cor. 15:7), and he became a highly esteemed man in the early Church, the leader at the Council of Jerusalem (Acts 15), and the author of the epistle bearing his name. (In the Roman traditions, this James is identified as **James the Less**, **May 3**.) He was martyred in AD 62. His symbol is a fuller's club, the final instrument of his death.

The symbols of James of Jerusalem are generally interchangeable with the symbols for James the Less. They include a saw, indicating that according to tradition he was dismembered. Other symbols include stones and a **fuller's club**, from the traditions that before he was dismembered, James was thrown from a wall of the Temple in Jerusalem, then stoned; and when he hadn't died, he was clubbed to death with a fuller's bat, and finally, his body was dismembered with a saw. Liturgical color: red.

October 28—Saint Simon and Saint Jude, Apostles

Tradition says these two apostles were martyred together in Persia, so they are commemorated together on the same date. Simon is identified as the Zealot (Matthew 10:4; Mark 3:18; Luke 6:15; Acts 1:13), possibly a reference to a first-century political group. (He should not be confused with Simon Peter.)

The Apostle Jude is mentioned only a few times as Judas (Luke 6:16; Acts 1:13) and once as "Judas, not Iscariot" (John 14:22). He is usually identified as Thaddeus, who is mentioned among the Twelve in Mark 3:18 and Matthew 10:3. (The author of the one-chapter epistle called the "Epistle of Jude" is Jude, the brother of James, and likely the brother of Jesus, not Jude the Apostle, honored on this day.)

Simon's symbol is a book with a fish resting on the top of it, to show that he became a fisher of men by the power of the Word of God. Jude may also be symbolized by a ship (for his missionary journeys) and a book (for his authorship of an epistle), and by symbols of his martyrdom: a lance, a club, or a halberd. Liturgical color: red.

October 31—Reformation Day

(Lutheran calendar.) This day celebrates the movement to reform the Roman Catholic Church that had its public beginnings on October 31, 1517, when Martin Luther posted his Ninety-Five Theses on the cathedral door in Wittenberg, Germany. This action sparked the debate that launched the **Protestant** Reformation. Liturgical color: red.

November 1—All Saints' Day

A major feast honoring those who have died in the faith. The word "saint" is the English translation of the Greek word *hagioi* (from *hagios*, "holy") and is used in Scripture to describe those called out of the world to be holy and set apart for God. It was a word applied to all followers of Christ, all members of his Church.

During the time of the persecutions in the early Church, those who had been killed for their faith (called **martyrs**, Greek for "witness") were honored for their sacrifice and were given the designation "saint." Those who had endured torture for their faith but had not died were called *confessors*. There is evidence that these martyrs were honored by a feast day (called "All Martyrs") from a very early time, ultimately resulting in the feast day known as All Saints' Day (at first celebrated on May 13, then moved to November 1 by the ninth century).

With the Reformation came a return to the scriptural understanding of saints as being the entire body of believers, all who have been sanctified by the **Holy Spirit**, with no distinctions made for a special class of believers. This also eliminated the distinction between All Saints' (**martyrs**) and **All Souls'** (faithful departed).

Today, All Saints' Day is a major feast in all churches, honoring all Christian saints, known and unknown.

November 2—All Souls' Day

(Roman calendar only.) Commemoration of All Faithful Departed. This feast has been celebrated since the eleventh century for the purpose of acknowledging and praying for Christians who have died, but are still in need of some purification before entering the presence of God. This is achieved through the **prayers** and good works of those still living. This intermediate state is called **purgatory** (from the same root word as "purge") in the Roman tradition, and just as the word suggests, there is a penal aspect to this state.

OLD TESTAMENT SAINTS & SYMBOLS
THE GENESIS ACCOUNTS

Creation

- **Creator's Star,** also called the *Star of David.* A six-pointed star whose six points recall the six days of creation.
- **Dove, hovering over waters.** The work of the Spirit of God in Creation (Gen. 1:1–2).

Adam and Eve

- **Garden of Eden.** Gardens represent a place of God's presence and abundance, and the Garden of Eden recalls the time of human innocence. The Garden of Eden contained two particular trees whose fruit was specifically forbidden to Adam and Eve: the tree of the knowledge of good and evil, and the tree of life, which offered everlasting life.
- **angel.** One of the cherubim posted at the gates of Eden after God banished Adam and Eve. He is shown with a flaming sword (Gen. 3:24).
- **apple.** In Latin the word for "apple" and for "evil" are identical: *malum*, which is the likely source of the tradition of the apple as the forbidden fruit of the Garden of Eden. The apple is the symbol of **the Fall** and **original sin.** When Christ is portrayed holding an apple, he is acknowledged as the Second Adam who brings life. When the Virgin Mary is portrayed holding an apple, she is the Second Eve.
- **dragon.** A large snakelike creature that represents the devil as well as sin, especially anger and envy. It also speaks of apostasy and heresy. A dragon is often portrayed being defeated by various saints, by Mary, or by Jesus Christ, to illustrate temptation resisted or Satan overcome. Sometimes a lion is shown slaying a dragon, symbolizing Jesus slaying Satan. The word for dragon is used in the Old

Testament to describe various large and frightening creatures and is translated in a variety of ways: "jackal," "sea-monster," "serpent," "whale," "wolf." In the New Testament, a dragon always refers to Satan, most especially the multiheaded beast in Revelation (Rev. 12:3, 4, 7, 9, 13, 16, 17; 13:2, 4, 11; 16:13; 20:2).

- **serpent.** The form Satan took as the tempter in Eden. Often shown coiled around a tree, with an apple.
- **shovel or spade.** Farming tools that represent Adam and the sweat of human labor that resulted from the Fall (Gen. 3:17–19).
- **spindle or distaff.** Weaving (household) tools that represent Eve and the sweat of human labor that resulted from the Fall (Gen. 3:17–19).

Cain and Abel

- **two altars.** Represent the two sacrifices, one of fruits and grains with the smoke winding downward, the second a lamb, with the smoke rising to God.
- **lamb on an altar.** Abel's sacrifice.
- **knotted club.** Represents Cain's killing of Abel.
- **plough.** Represents Cain's work as a farmer, which was withheld from him as punishment for Abel's murder.
- **shepherd's crook or staff**. Represents Abel's work keeping flocks.

Noah and the Great Deluge (Gen. 6:5–9:19)

- **ark.** The boat built by Noah to save his family and all living creatures from destruction and the most common symbol of the Flood. By extension a symbol of salvation. Peter likens the ark to Holy Baptism (1 Pet. 3:20–21).
- **dove, carrying an olive leaf** (Gen. 8:11). The bird sent out by Noah. It returned with an olive leaf in its mouth, evidence that the flood waters had receded. Also represents new life, peace, and forgiveness.

- **raven** (Gen. 8:6–7). First bird sent out by Noah to determine if the flood waters had receded. Since the raven did not return to the ark, the raven is said to be a symbol of unrest, or the indifferent and unrepentant sinner.
- **rainbow** (Gen. 9:12–17). With or without ark. God's covenant with Noah never again to destroy the earth by flood. Often Jesus is depicted seated on a rainbow in representations of the Last Judgment.

The Tower of Babel (Gen. 11:1–9)
- A ziggurat-style building built with the intention of reaching heaven. Represents sinful arrogance. (A ziggurat was a temple constructed in the style of a terraced pyramid, common in ancient Mesopotamia.)

Abraham the Patriarch:
Melchizedek (Gen. 14:18–20; Ps. 110:4; Heb. 5:6–10; 6:20; 7) The King of Salem who was also a priest of the God Most High. He brought bread and wine to Abraham (Abram) following a great military victory and blessed him.
- **crown and censer.** Symbols of king and priest.
- **scepter and censer.** Symbols of king and priest.
- **chalice and loaf.** Symbolizes the bread and wine Melchizedek served Abraham (Abram) and his life as a type of Jesus Christ.
- **crown and mitre.** Symbols of king and priest.

The Call of Abraham (Gen. 12:1–3; 15:5–6)
- **stars.** A number of stars in a blue field symbolize God's promise to Abraham (Abram): I will make you a great nation; your descendants will be as the stars of the heavens. One star is bigger than the rest, representing Messiah.

The Sacrifice of Isaac (Gen. 22:1–19)
- **brazier of burning coal, with wood and knife.** Implements of sacrifice.
- **knife.** For sacrifice.

- **ram.** The substitute sacrifice.
- **wood.** Isaac carried the wood for this sacrifice and is symbolized by bundles of wood in the shape of a cross.

Esau
- **bow and arrows.** Symbolizes Esau as a great hunter.
- **bowl, with pottage or stew.** ("Pottage" is King James English for lentil stew.) That for which Esau traded his birthright (Gen. 25:29–34).

Jacob
- **arm, hairy.** Symbol of Jacob's deception of Isaac (Gen. 27:1–29).
- **ladder.** Jacob's dream and his vision of the ladder going into heaven (Gen. 28:10–22).
- **sun, moon, and twelve stars.** Jacob and his family, a symbol taken from the imagery of Joseph's dream (Gen. 37:9).

Joseph
- **coat of many colors.** A richly ornamented coat, a gift to Joseph from his doting father Jacob and the cause of great jealousy among his brothers (Gen. 37:3–4).
- **sheaf of grain standing upright, while others bow to it.** Joseph and his brothers, per Joseph's dream (Gen. 37:5–8).
- **sun, moon, and eleven stars, bowing to Joseph.** Jacob and his family, bowing to Joseph, per Joseph's dream (Gen 37:9).
- **pit or cistern.** Symbolizes the betrayal of Joseph's brothers when they beat him up, threw him into a pit, and eventually sold him to slave traders (Gen. 37:18–28).
- **scepter and chain.** Represents Joseph's advancement to a position of authority and power in Egypt.
- **Egyptian images**, such as a **pyramid**, a **Sphinx**, or an **Egyptian column** represent Joseph's time in Egypt.
- **mummy.** Represents the deaths of Jacob and later Joseph. Both were embalmed for burial according to Egyptian custom, but their remains were returned to Canaan for burial (Gen. 50:1–14, 24–26; Josh. 24:32).

Jacob blesses his sons (Genesis 49:1–27)
His final prophetic benedictions upon his sons:

- **Reuben** (Gen. 49:3–4). Symbol: water, for turbulence and indecision.
- **Simeon and Levi** (Gen. 49:5–7). Symbol: sword for violence, anger, and cruelty.
- **Judah** (Gen. 49:8–12). Symbol: lion's whelp, for sovereignty, strength, and courage. Later his descendant Jesus would be called the Lion of the tribe of Judah. Also symbolized by a scepter, for his acquired position as leader.
- **Zebulun** (Gen. 49:13). Symbol: ship in harbor.
- **Issachar** (Gen. 49:14–15). Symbol: donkey with two burdens.
- **Dan** (Gen. 49:16–18). Symbol: serpent, or viper.
- **Gad** (Gen. 49:19). Symbol: implements of war, banner.
- **Asher** (Gen. 49:20). Symbol: a horn of plenty or cornucopia for bounty.
- **Naphtali** (Gen. 49:21). Symbol: a running doe (hind).
- **Joseph** (Gen. 49:22–26). Symbol: fruitful bough over well or spring.
- **Benjamin** (Gen. 49:27). Symbol: wolf.

MOSES AND THE EXODUS

Israel in Bondage in Egypt
- **whip with a pile of bricks.** The Israelite slaves were forced to make bricks and collect the straw for them as well (Ex. 5:6–9).
- **pyramids.** Traditional symbols of Egypt.

The Life of Moses
- **basket in bulrushes.** Moses rescued from death by his creative mother (Ex. 2:1–10).
- **shepherd's crook or staff.** Moses' life as a shepherd or herdsman for his father-in-law (Ex. 3:1).
- **burning bush.** The call of Moses (Ex. 3:1–10).

The Exodus

- **serpent and staff.** One of the miracles of Moses and Aaron before Pharaoh, when they threw a staff on the floor and it turned into a snake, and then returned to its original form when they picked it up (Ex. 4:1–5).
- **ten plagues.** The plagues called down on Egypt when the Pharaoh refused to allow the Israelites to leave Egypt and slavery.

  water turning to blood (Ex. 7:14–24)
  frogs (Ex. 8:1–15)
  gnats (or lice) (Ex. 8:16–19)
  flies (Ex. 8:20–24)
  death of livestock (Ex. 9:1–7)
  boils (Ex. 9:8–12)
  hail (Ex. 9:18–34)
  locusts (Ex. 10:3–20)
  darkness (Ex. 10:21–23)
  death of the firstborn (Ex. 11:4–7; 12:12, 29–30).

- **door jambs sprinkled with blood.** The LORD went throughout Egypt to kill the firstborn, but when he saw this sign, he passed over these homes (Ex. 12:1–13).
- **two tables of stone.** The Ten Commandments or Decalogue (Greek). The Law given by the LORD to Moses not once, but twice (Exodus 20, 34) after the first set was shattered by Moses, who was angered by the people's casting and worshiping the golden calf. The second set was stored in or near the Ark of the Covenant along with Aaron's budded staff and a jar of manna.

  Shown with the numbers one through ten written in Roman numerals. May be shown in various configurations, based on different traditions. The Jewish practice is five on each tablet. Catholics and Lutherans will have three on the first tablet and seven on the second. Reformed churches generally show four on the first tablet and six on the second.

- **rock, with water gushing from it.** Moses struck the rock in the wilderness and water poured out for the people (Ex. 17:5–6).

Aaron
- **budding rod.** Divine confirmation of Aaron's priesthood (Num. 17:6–11). This rod was placed in or near the Ark of the Covenant along with the jar of manna and the tables of the Ten Commandments.
- **golden calf.** The idol built by Aaron at the insistence of the Israelites in Moses' absence (Exodus 32).
- **breastplate.** Symbolic of his position as high priest (Exodus 28) and of priesthood in general.
- **golden censer.** On the Day of Atonement, Aaron carried a censer filled with burning coals and incense into the Holy of Holies. The smoke of the incense masked the Ark and the Presence of God so he wouldn't die.

Miriam
- **tambourine.** Recalls her dance and song of joy after the Israelites' escape from Egypt (Ex. 15:20–21).

OLD TESTAMENT WORSHIP

Furniture of the Tabernacle and Temple
- **Ark of the Covenant** or the Ark of the Testimony. The single piece of furniture in the Most Holy Place (Holy of Holies). A small chestlike structure, constructed of acacia wood and covered in gold inside and out. In it were stored the stone tablets containing the Law given to Moses by the LORD, a jar of manna, and Aaron's staff that had budded. On the lid was a gold atonement cover (KJV: mercy seat) where the blood of the sacrifices on the **Day of Atonement** were sprinkled. Flanking the atonement cover were two gold cherubim kneeling toward the center with their wings stretched over the cover. As the Ark was the location of the Presence of God himself, it was the holiest of all holy places.

- **altar of incense.** One of the three pieces of furniture in the Holy Place (Ex. 30:1–6). Incense was to be burned morning and evening by the priest as he tended the lamps. This altar was also anointed with sacrificial blood on the **Day of Atonement**. Incense represents the prayers rising to the Lord:

    May my prayer be set before you like incense;
    may the lifting up of my hands be like the evening
    sacrifice. (Ps. 141:2)

- **table for the bread of the Presence** (KJV: *showbread* or *shewbread*). One of three pieces of furniture in the Holy Place. A gold-covered table on which twelve loaves of bread were displayed, freshly made every week. Represented the twelve tribes of Israel and their everlasting covenant with the LORD (Lev. 24:5–9).

- **lampstand** with seven lamps (*menorah*). One of the three pieces of furniture in the Holy Place. Cast of pure gold, these lights were to be tended at all times by the priest (Lev. 24:1–4). Represents the glory of the LORD, and that he is the light.

- **bronze basin, sea,** or **laver.** Sometimes the word "brazen" is used instead of bronze. Stood in the outer court, before the entrance to the Holy Place (the Tent of Meeting). Large bronze basin to hold water that the priests used for cleansing before approaching the Tent of Meeting—where the LORD met his people (Ex. 30:17–21).

- **altar of burnt offering**. Stood in the outer court of the Tabernacle where public worship took place. This was a bronze altar upon which sacrifices were made and at which all gifts were presented. It is the point of atonement and reconciliation with God (Ex. 27:1–8).

Feasts and Fasts

- **Sabbath** (Hebrew, *Shabbat*). (Lev. 23:3.) The weekly day of rest and worship for Israel, taken from the account of Creation, where God rested on the seventh day (Gen. 2:2–3).

- **Feast of Passover** (Hebrew, *Pesakh* or Greek, *Pascha*). The first of the holy days prescribed by God, commemorating his deliverance of Israel from their slavery in Egypt. Held in the first month of the religious year. Celebrated by cleansing the home of all leaven, and sharing a leisurely family feast that includes recounting the Exodus story in food and word. Symbol: unleavened bread and a cup of wine. The **Last Supper** of Jesus with his disciples before his death was a Passover meal and was ordained by him as the foundation for the Lord's Supper or Eucharist (Matt. 26:26–28; Mark 14:12–25; Luke 22:7–20). Paul calls Jesus our Passover lamb (1 Cor. 5:7–8), a designation carried over into the Christian liturgy.

- **Feast of Unleavened Bread** (Hebrew, *Hag HaMatzot*). (Lev. 23:5–8.) A seven-day feast that follows the Feast of Passover, continuing the ban on leaven and the memorial of the Exodus. One of the three annual pilgrimage feasts which all men were required to attend. Symbol: unleavened bread and a cup of wine.

- **The Day of First Fruits** (Hebrew, *Yom HaBikkurim* or *Sfirat Haomer*). (Lev. 23:9–14.) Held the third day from Passover, during the Feast of Unleavened Bread. Honored the earliest harvest, which was barley. Sheaves of grain waved by the priests as thanksgiving for the harvest were sometimes called a *wave offering*. Symbol: a sheaf of grain.

- **The Feast of Weeks,** or **Pentecost** (Hebrew, *Shavuot*). (Lev. 23:15–21.) Harvest festival held fifty days after the Day of First Fruits, celebrating the wheat harvest. Rather than sheaves of grain, worshipers offered loaves of leavened bread made from the ripe grain of the new harvest which were waved by the priests. In later Judaism this feast came to include a commemoration of Moses receiving the law on Mount Sinai. One of the three annual pilgrimage feasts which all men were required to attend. Symbol: a sheaf of wheat with a symbol of the Law: a **scroll**, a roll of parchment, or **stone tablets**.

- **The Feast of Trumpets** (Hebrew, *Rosh HaShanah*). (Lev. 23:23–24.) The first day of the seventh month of the religious calendar is the first day of the civil year, and is treated like New Year's Day. This day of rest was marked by the blowing of trumpets (*shofar* or *ram's horn*). Symbol: a ram's horn (trumpet).

- **The Day of Atonement** (Hebrew, *Yom Kippur*). (Lev. 23:26–32; Ex. 30:10.) One of the holiest days of the Jewish calendar, a day of fasting and repentance for one's sins. In biblical times, a sacrifice was brought to the tabernacle or Temple to atone for one's sins. With the destruction of the Temple, this day became a fast, on the order of Isaiah 58:5. Symbol: a goat, the sacrifice for atonement.

- **The Feast of the Tabernacles** (Hebrew, *Sukkot*) or the Feast of Booths, or the Feast of the Ingathering. (Lev. 23:33–36; Deut 16:13.) A seven-day festival held at the completion of the harvests of the fields, orchards, and vines, and one of the three major pilgrimage festivals which all men were required to attend. Often called the festival of booths because everyone was required to live in a booth constructed of tree branches for the entirety of the feast, recalling their sojourn in the wilderness and their temporary shelters after the Exodus from Egypt. Symbol: a tent or shelter made with tree boughs.

- **The Feast of Esther** (Hebrew, *Purim*). From the book of Esther, an account of the Jewish people in the postexilic period. The word *purim* means "lots" from the lots that were cast by Haman (Esth. 3:7) to set the date on which all the Jews in the Persian kingdom were to be killed. It is a feast instituted by Mordecai (Esth. 9:19–28), to be celebrated with great joy, feasting, and laughter. Symbols: a crown (Queen Esther), gifts, party noisemakers, and food, such as *Hamantashen* cookies.

- **The Feast of Dedication** (Hebrew, *Hanukkah*). An extrabiblical feast (though mentioned in John's Gospel, John 10:22) instituted by Judas Maccabeus in 164 BC to commemorate the cleansing and rededication of the Temple after it had been defiled by Antiochus Epiphanes, a ruler of the Seleucid Empire. The symbol is a lighted **menorah** with nine lights (or *Hanukkah lamp*), for the miracle of provision in which one day's worth of consecrated oil lasted for eight days.

THE JUDGES

Promised Land

- **grapes.** Large and lush, carried on a pole. Evidence brought back from Canaan by Joshua and Caleb and ten other spies (Num. 13:17–27), proving the truth of God's promise that they would be given a fertile and productive land (Deut. 8:7–9).
- **comb of honey and a vessel of milk.** The returning spies described the Canaan as "flowing with milk and honey" (Num. 13:27).

Joshua

- **scepter and trumpet.** Successor to Moses; spiritual and military leader (Num. 27:18–23).
- **sword and trumpet.** Joshua's military victory over the city of Jericho (Josh. 6).

Gideon

- **fleece, with bowl.** Gideon tests the Lord (Judg. 6:36–40).
- **light or torch** with pitcher. Gideon rousts the Midianites through a strategy from the LORD (Judg. 7:15–22).

Ruth

- **wisp of wheat.** The grain Ruth gleaned, left behind by the harvesters (Ruth 2:1–3).

Samson

- **lion.** Ripped apart by Samson, evidence of his strength (Judg. 14:5–6).

- **jawbone of an ass.** Used by Samson to kill 1000 Philistines (Judg. 15:13–17).
- **seven cords**. Used by Delilah in her plot to discover the source of Samson's strength (Judg. 16:6–9).
- **two columns out of plumb.** Symbolizes Samson's last feat of strength, when he pushed out the pillars of the temple to Dagon and brought the roof crashing down (Judg. 16:21–30).

THE ACCOUNT OF THE KINGS

David
- **harp or lyre.** Represents David's gift for music, which could soothe and comfort (1 Sam. 16:23). The book of Psalms contains many songs attributed to David.
- **horn of oil.** A symbol of David's anointing to be king (1 Sam. 16:1–15).
- **shepherd's crook or staff.** Symbolic of David's early life as a shepherd. Reminder of Psalm 23, the Shepherd's Psalm.
- **lion.** Killed by David while he was a shepherd, showing his courage and strength (1 Sam. 17:34–37).
- **sling, with five stones.** The weapon David used to kill the Philistine giant Goliath (1 Sam. 17:40–50).
- **head of Goliath.** David's victory over the Philistine giant Goliath (1 Sam. 17:50–51).
- **Shield of David** (Hebrew, *Mogen David*). The six-pointed star of David, sometimes called the Seal of Solomon. The symbol for Judaism and Jewish identity since the Middle Ages. The ancient symbol for Judaism is the **menorah**.

Solomon
- **scroll with a scepter.** Solomon as both king and author.
- **Temple** (model of). Solomon as builder of the first Temple.
- **Temple, under construction.** Solomon as builder of the first Temple.

THE PROPHETS

Elijah (1 Kings 17:1–2 Kings 2:11)

Elijah is the forerunner, the prophet of all prophets. It is Elijah who appears with Moses at the Transfiguration of Jesus. It is Elijah whose appearance Israel awaits, symbolized especially in the Passover meal, with a chair left empty for the prophet and a child who goes to the door to see if Elijah has come. In the Gospels, the crowds often asked if John the Baptist was Elijah, and when Jesus asked Peter, "Who do they say that I am?" he replied, "Some say Elijah."

- **raven or bird carrying food or bread.** The miracle of God's provision when he sent birds to feed Elijah (1 Kings 17:1–6).
- **cruse of oil.** The miracle of the inexhaustible supply of oil and flour needed to feed a widow and her son (1 Kings 17:8–16).
- **red vestment and scroll.** The scroll symbolizes Elijah as prophet of God. The red vestment (as worn at Pentecost) represents the occasion when Elijah challenged the prophets of Baal, and called down fire from heaven to consume their sacrifices (1 Kings 18:25–29).
- **mantle.** Elijah gave his mantle (or cloak) to Elisha signaling that he would take Elijah's place as a prophet (1 Kings 19:19–21).
- **fiery chariot.** Elijah was carried into heaven in a fiery chariot (2 Kings 2:11). Prefigures the Ascension of Christ.

Elisha

- **double-headed eagle or dove.** Represents perhaps Elisha's request that he inherit a double portion of Elijah's spirit (2 Kings 2:9).
- **Elijah's mantle.** Given to Elisha to signify that he would take Elijah's place (1 Kings 19:19–21).

THE FOUR MAJOR PROPHETS

So named for the length of their writings, not simply the importance of their message.

Isaiah

- **burning coal held in tongs.** Isaiah's purification and call (Isa. 6:6–9).

Jeremiah

- **cistern.** Jeremiah was imprisoned in an empty water cistern for his preaching (Jer. 38:6).
- **potter's wheel.** From Jeremiah's teaching about God's power and purposes (Jer. 18:3–10).
- **stone.** Jeremiah is said to have died by stoning.

Ezekiel

- **gate, closed or turreted.** Symbolic of Ezekiel's vision of Jerusalem under siege (Ezekiel 4–5).
- **plan of the New Temple.** From Ezekiel's vision of the New Temple (Ezekiel 40–46).
- **tetramorph.** A figure with four heads and eight wings and with fiery wheels underfoot (Ezek. 1:4–24). Also a symbol of the Four **Evangelists**.

Daniel

- **giant image.** The large statue that appeared in Nebuchadnezzar's dream, which only Daniel could reveal and interpret (Daniel 2). Represents Daniel as the interpreter of dreams.
- **lion.** Daniel refused to worship the idols of Babylon and was thrown into a den of hungry lions. Represents his faith and courage (Daniel 6).
- **ram with four horns.** Symbolic of Daniel's visions (Dan. 8:8).

THE MINOR PROPHETS

Hosea

- **mantle, cast off.** Represents Hosea's message of God's love cast off by Israel (Hos. 4:1–3).
- **broken idol.** From Hosea's message that Israel forsake its idols and repent (Hos. 14).
- **trumpet.** A warning of impeding destruction (Hos. 8:1).
- **lion.** The promise of utter destruction for the unfaithful (Hos. 5:14).

Joel

- **hood (pointed).** Speaks perhaps of Joel's call for fasting and repentance by donning sackcloth (Joel 1:13–14).
- **trumpet.** A sound of alarm (Joel 2:1) or a call to gather the faithful (Joel 2:15–16).

Amos

- **shepherd's crook or staff.** Amos had two jobs: he was a shepherd and he also tended a sycamore fig grove (Amos 7:14–15). This symbol reflects his work as a shepherd.

Obadiah

The symbols of the prophet Obadiah find their source in a story about another Obadiah, a godly man who served the wicked King Ahab.

- **two caves.** When Ahab ordered the prophets of the Lord killed, Obadiah saved them by hiding one hundred of them in two caves (1 Kings 18:3–16).
- **pitcher with loaves.** Symbolizes the water and bread that Obadiah supplied to the hidden prophets (1 Kings 18:13).

Jonah

- **great fish.** Jonah was swallowed by a great fish when he tried to avoid God's instructions to go to Nineveh to preach repentance (Jonah 1–2).

- **gourd.** Jonah's only comfort when to his dismay, Nineveh repented (Jonah 4).

Micah

- **temple on a mountain.** From Micah's prophecy of hope for Jerusalem (Mic. 4:1–2).
- **broken sword and lance (spear).** From Micah's prophecy (Mic. 4:3):

    He will judge between many peoples
    and will settle disputes for strong nations far and wide.
    They will beat their swords into plowshares
    and their spears into pruning hooks.
    Nation will not take up sword against nation,
    nor will they train for war anymore.

Nahum

- **feet of an angel emerging from clouds on mountain top.** From Nahum's encouraging words (Nah. 1:15):

    Look, there on the mountains,
    the feet of one who brings good news,
    who proclaims peace!
    Celebrate your festivals, O Judah,
    and fulfill your vows.
    No more will the wicked invade you;
    they will be completely destroyed.

- **broken yoke.** God promises to deliver Judah from bondage and the threat of captivity (Nah. 1:13).

Habakkuk

- **model of the Temple.** From his words (Hab. 2:20) sounded as a call to worship for centuries:

    But the LORD is in his holy temple;
    let all the earth be silent before him.

Zephaniah

- **walled city with sword hanging above it.** Zephaniah's prophetic message of God's wrath awaiting Jerusalem and the nations (Zeph. 1:14–18).

Haggai

- **Temple under construction**. From Haggai's message encouraging the people of Jerusalem to rebuild the Temple (Hag 1:1–11; 2:1–19).
- **timbers.** From Haggai's message challenging the people of Jerusalem to cease working on their own homes and begin to rebuild the Temple (Hag. 1:3–4, 7–8).

Zechariah

- **measuring line.** A tool used in building, hence a symbol of restoration (Zechariah 2; also Jer. 31:38–40; Ezek. 40:3).
- **stone full of eyes.** Symbolizes God's wisdom, that he is in control of people, nations, and events (Zech. 3:9; 4:10).
- **winged scroll.** The word of God going out, able to be read by all (Zech. 5:1–4).
- **donkey.** A messianic prophecy regarding Jesus' triumphant entry into Jerusalem riding a donkey (Zech. 9:9). See **Palm Sunday**.

Malachi

- **angel issuing from clouds.** God's messenger coming to prepare the way for the return of the LORD (Mal. 3:1). Angels are messengers, as are prophets and priests. Jesus stated that this prophecy was fulfilled by **John the Baptist** (Matt. 11:10).

FIVE

Liturgical Worship

Christian worship is never a solitary undertaking. Both on its visible and invisible sides, it has a thoroughly social and organic character. The worshiper, however lonely in appearance, comes before God as a member of a great family; part of the Communion of Saints, living and dead. His own small effort of adoration is offered "in and for all." (Evelyn Underhill)[25]

RITES

celebration. The solemn performance of a religious ceremony, such as **Holy Communion**.

Eucharist Office. The prescribed form or service of worship. If capitalized, refers to the **Divine Office**. Also called simply the *Office*.

liturgical. Refers to formal worship, particularly worship in churches that follow a specific **liturgy**.

liturgy. (Greek, "public service.") All the material authorized by the church as suitable for use at its public services. Sometimes used specifically to mean the Liturgy of the Eucharist.

order. The prescribed form of a service, as the Order for **Matins**, the Order for **Vespers**, the Order for the Baptism of Infants, etc.

Ordinary of the Mass or **ordinary.** Those parts of the service that remain constant from week to week, in contrast with those parts that vary according to the ecclesiastical calendar. These include *Kyrie eleison*, *Gloria in excelsis*, the **Creed**, the **Canon**, the **Lord's Prayer**, the *Agnus Dei*.

Propers of the Mass or **Propers.** (Latin, "appropriate to.") The variable parts of the service, which change according to the day of the church year. Before Vatican II, the Propers included the **Introit**, **Collect**, **Epistle**, **Gradual**, and Gospel. Today the Propers include entrance antiphon, the **Opening Prayer** or **Collect**, the chant after the first reading, the **Preface**, the **Prayer over the Gifts**, the **Communion Antiphon**, and the **Prayer after Communion**. The Propers may be found in the **missal**, **The Book of Common Prayer**, or in a service booklet.

- **Introit.** (Latin, "to enter.") The introit was composed of verses from the Psalms, sung near the beginning of the service, and followed by the *Gloria Patri*. The introit often gave a particular Sunday its name. In today's **Mass**, an entrance hymn is sung followed by the entrance antiphon.
- **Collect.** A brief formal prayer used in Western liturgies and said before the Epistle. The collect varies with the day and focuses on a single theme, usually tied to the Epistle and Gospel appointed to the day. Its name is derived from the concept that the petitions of the members of the **congregation** are "collected" into a single prayer by the **priest**. Some collects have been in use for 1,500 years, rooted in their Latin originals.

rite. A religious order of service, such as the rite of confirmation. Also, a distinct and historic liturgical family, such as the Roman rite, the Byzantine rite, the Alexandrian rite, etc.

ritual. The prescribed form of a ceremony.

SERVICES

confessional service. A preparatory service of public confession of sins preceding the **Holy Communion**.

contemporary worship. Services in the modern idiom often accompanied by guitar or other musical instruments.

Liturgy of the Hours. The daily public prayer of the church for praising God and sanctifying the Day. Also known as the *Divine Office* or the *Daily Office,* the Liturgy of the Hours is largely celebrated by clergy and religious orders, although the laity have been encouraged to participate as well. The liturgy is celebrated at fixed hours of the day, which are known as *canonical hours.* The traditional hours are:
- **Matins**, sung or recited about midnight. (Often called *Nocturns* in medieval texts, after the specific readings of the office.)
- **Lauds**, sung or recited about 3 AM.
- **Prime**, sung or recited at the first hour of the day, or sunrise.
- **Terce**, sung or recited at the third hour of the day, or about 9 AM.
- **Sext**, sung or recited at the sixth hour of the day, or about midday.
- **Nones**, sung or recited at the ninth hour of the day, or about 3 PM.
- **Vespers**, the liturgical office of the evening, sometimes called *Evensong.*
- **Compline**, the last service of the day, about 9 PM.

In the medieval church, each of these hours symbolized an event in the Passion of our Lord.
- Matins: Jesus before Caiaphas.
- Lauds: Jesus condemned by Caiaphas.
- Prime: His appearance before Pilate.
- Terce: The scourging and crowning with thorns.
- Sext: Jesus on the cross, and the **Seven Last Words** of Christ.
- Nones: Death of the Savior.

119

- Vespers: His deposition and entombment.
- Compline: The watch set at the tomb.

In 1549, the Church of England reduced the Daily Office to *Morning Prayer* (Matins) and *Evening Prayer* (Evensong) in the new **Book of Common Prayer**.

With Vatican II, the hours of the Daily Office in the Roman tradition that are to be observed are: Vespers (evening prayer) and Lauds (morning prayer), now designated as the chief hours of prayer; Compline, to mark the close of day; the Office of Readings, which was formerly Matins; and one of the minor hours, Terce, Sext, or None. Prime is no longer celebrated. The offices of the Liturgy of the Hours are outlined in the **breviary**.

Mass. (Latin, *missa*, "to send.") The traditional name of the Eucharist. From the Old Latin dismissal rite: *ite, missa est* or "Go, the Mass is [ended]."

mystery play. A religious drama from medieval times, particularly popular during the celebration of Corpus Christi, based on stories from the Bible. Dramas from the liturgy of **Holy Week** and **Easter** were called *passion plays*; dramas with an ethical theme were called *morality plays*; dramas based on the life of a saint were called *miracle plays*. These plays related Bible stories and sacred themes in local languages, unlike the liturgy, which was offered in Latin.

occasional services. Those conducted for special needs such as **baptism**, dedication, burial, **confirmation**, marriage.

preaching mission. A series of services led by a missioner with the intention of creating a spiritual **revival** among the people. Sometimes called *revival meeting*.

retreat. A withdrawal from the world for a short period of **meditation** and spiritual revival. The duration is usually several days to a week.

vigil. The service held on the evening before an important day, such as the service held on **Christmas Eve** or **Holy Saturday**.

LITURGICAL RESPONSES

Responses are short sentences said by the **congregation** in response to those spoken by the **priest**.

alleluia. (The Anglicized form of *Hallelujah*, Hebrew for "Praise ye Jehovah" or "Praise ye the Lord.") A salutation of praise to God, especially the response sung before the Gospel in the Eucharistic service. During Lent, the Alleluia is not sung; instead, a **tract** (selected verses from the Psalms) is used.

> *O the happiness of the heavenly alleluia, sung in security, in fear of no adversity! We shall have no enemies in heaven, we shall never lose a friend. God's praises are sung both there and here, but here they are sung in anxiety, there, in security; here they are sung by those destined to die, there, by those destined to live for ever; here they are sung in hope, there, in hope's fulfillment; here they are sung by wayfarers, there, by those living in their own country.*
>
> *So let us sing now, not in order to enjoy a life of leisure, but in order to lighten our labors. You should sing as wayfarers do—sing, but continue your journey. Do not be lazy, but sing to make your journey more enjoyable. Sing, but keep going.* (Augustine)[26]

amen. (Hebrew, translated by Luther as "Yea, yea, it shall be so.") A response indicating assent, said or sung at the end of prayers, **hymns**, and **anthems**.

doxology. (Greek, "to speak praise.") Words of praise to God, either sung or said, as the conclusion of the *Lord's Prayer*, the *Gloria in Excelsis*, and the *Gloria Patri*. The most familiar doxology is the response sung in many churches at the Presentation of the Gifts (**Offering**):

Praise God, from whom all blessings flow.
Praise Him, all creatures here below.
Praise Him above, ye heavenly hosts.
Praise Father, Son, and Holy Ghost. Amen.

Gloria Patri. (Latin, "Glory be to the Father.") Praise to the Trinity, sung after the Psalm. Sometimes called the Lesser Doxology. The complete text is:

Glory be to the Father and to the Son and to the Holy Spirit,
As it was in the beginning, is now, and ever shall be,
world without end. Amen.

Gloria tibi. (Latin, "Glory be to Thee.") The congregational response after the announcement of the Gospel lesson in the Eucharistic service. The complete sentence is *Gloria tibi, Domine* or "Glory to you, Lord Christ."

hosanna. (Hebrew, "save now.") The shout of the throng on Palm Sunday, which became the conclusion of the **Sanctus**.

Laus tibi. (Latin, "Praise to Thee.") The congregational response after the reading of the Gospel lesson. The complete sentence is *Laus tibi, Domine* or "Praise to you, Lord Christ."

tract. Verses from the Psalms used in place of **Alleluia** during Lent.

versicles. (Latin, "a little verse.") Short verses from the Psalms read antiphonally by the **minister** and **congregation**.

PRAYERS OF THE PEOPLE

General Intercessions or **Prayers of the Faithful** or **Prayers of the People.** A time of prayer or **intercession** in the liturgy in which the needs of the **congregation**, the Church, and the world are brought before God (1 Tim. 2:1–2). These usually take the form of a **litany**, in which the **officiant** offers a specific request, and following a short time of silence for individual prayer, the people respond in accordance with the form used. These prayers may also be called *Bidding Prayers* in the Anglican tradition. An especially solemn form of General Intercession is used on **Good Friday**.

intercession. To pray on behalf of others.

invocation. (Latin, "to call upon.") (1) The announcement at the beginning of the service invoking God's presence "In the Name of the Father, and of the Son, and of the Holy Spirit." (2) A prayer invoking the blessing of God.

litany. (Greek, "intercessory prayer.") A form of prayer in which petitions are uttered by the **pastor**, and the **congregation** responds with a refrain after each, such as, "Hear us, O Lord." The oldest form of litany is the *Kyrie eleison.*

The Lord's Prayer. The prayer Christ taught his disciples as the model for praying (Matt. 6:9–13; Luke 11:2–4). Used at almost every service, it has become the best known and most beloved Christian prayer in the world. The now-familiar doxology included with the prayer in the Anglican and **Protestant** traditions was not part of the prayer as taught by Jesus, but first appeared in the form we know in the earliest editions of the Anglican **Book of Common Prayer**. A similar doxology is part of the Lord's Prayer presented in the *Didache*, or The Teachings of the Twelve Apostles, a first-century collection of teachings addressed to gentile converts. Some think this doxology was added when the Lord's Prayer was used in liturgy, and simply found its way into the English Bible because of its familiarity. This doxology is not used in the Roman church. Sometimes called the "Our Father" or *Pater Noster* (Latin, "Our Father").

Our Father, who art in heaven,
    hallowed be thy Name,
    thy kingdom come,
    thy will be done,
        on earth as it is in heaven.
Give us this day our daily bread.
And forgive us our trespasses,
    as we forgive those
        who trespass against us.
And lead us not into temptation,
    but deliver us from evil.
[For thine is the kingdom,
    and the power, and the glory,
    for ever and ever. Amen.][27]

salutation. (Latin, "greeting.") The **pastor's** greeting to the **congregation**, "The Lord be with you," and their response, "And with thy spirit" or "And also with you." This salutation is given before **prayers** and **benedictions**.

silent prayer. The worshipers' private devotions before and after the service.

suffrages. Short intercessory petitions in a prayer or litany.

thanksgiving. The offering of praise to God for his goodness and mercy.

Prayer is a profound act of worship, that asks neither why nor wherefore. It rises like beauty, like sweetness, like love. The more there is in it of love, the more of sacrifice. And when the fire has wholly consumed the sacrifice, a sweet savour ascends. (Romano Guardini)[28]

ORDER OF SERVICE

Sunday Mass (Roman)	**Anglican**[29]
Introductory Rite (including penitential rite)	Beginning of Mass (Greeting)
Entrance Song	Introductory Rites
Greeting	Procession/Introit
Rite of Blessing and Sprinkling Holy Water, or Penitential Rite	Sign of the Cross and Greeting
	The Word of God
Kyrie eleison	Collect for Purity
Gloria in excelsis	[The Summary of the Law]
Opening Prayer	Canticles
Liturgy of the Word	*Kyrie eleison* or *Trisagion*
First Reading	*Gloria in excelsis*
Gradual	The Collect of the Day
Responsorial Psalm	The Lessons
Second Reading	The Sermon
Alleluia or Gospel Acclamation	The Nicene Creed
Gospel	The Prayers of the People
Homily	Confession of Sin
Profession of Faith	[Exhortation]
General Intercessions	General Confession
Liturgy of the Eucharist	Absolution
Preparation of the Altar and Gifts	[Comfortable Words]
Prayer over the Gifts	The Peace
Preface	The Holy Communion
Sanctus	Offertory
Eucharistic Prayer	Doxology
Communion Rite	Prayer over Gifts
Lord's Prayer	The Great Thanksgiving
Doxologue	Dialogue
Sign of Peace	Preface
Breaking of the Bread	*Sanctus*
Communion	Eucharistic Prayer
Communion Song	The Lord's Prayer
Period of Silence or Song	The Breaking of the Bread
Prayer after Communion	Distribution of Bread and Wine
Concluding Rite	Postcommunion Prayer
Greeting	Recessional
Blessing	Blessing
Dismissal	Dismissal

THE FIRST PRAYER ON SUNDAYS

We ask for your help, Father of Christ, Lord of all that is, Creator of all the created, maker of all that is made; we stretch out clean hands to you and lay bare our minds, Lord, before you.

Have mercy, we pray you; spare us, be kind to us, improve us; fill us with virtue, faith and knowledge.

Look at us, Lord; we bring our weaknesses for you to see. Be kind and merciful to all of us here gathered together; have pity on this people of yours and show them your favor, make them equitable, temperate and pure; send out angelic powers to make this your people—all that compose it—holy and noble.

Send the Holy Spirit into our minds, I beg you, and grant that we may learn to understand the holy scriptures he inspired. May we interpret them correctly and fittingly, for the benefit of all the faithful here present.

Through your only Son, Jesus Christ, in the Holy Spirit. Through him may glory and power be yours, now and age after age. Amen.

(The Euchologium of Serapion)[30]

All the following definitions of different parts of the liturgy are presented in the order in which they appear in the liturgy.

INTRODUCTORY RITES

prelude. Organ music played before the opening of the service while the worshipers are arriving, designed to create an atmosphere of worship.

entrance hymn. The **hymn** sung during the **procession.** May be called the *processional hymn.*

PROCESSION

In liturgical traditions, there may be as many as four processions in a service: the Entrance, the Gospel, the Offertory, and the Communion procession. The service begins with an entrance procession, which may be as simple as a server or two followed by a priest, or may include many servers, the choir, and the clergy.

THE ORDER FOR THE PROCESSION

May my song rise like incense in thy presence. And for us may it be a perfume of consolation, of goodness and grace, so that these fumes will drive out every phantom from the mind and body, leaving us, as the Apostle Paul phrased it, smelling sweetly of God. May all the attacks of demons fly from this incense, like dust before the wind, like smoke before the dancing flames. (Anglo-Saxon blessing of incense)[31]

Below is the order for participants in a procession:
* **thurifer** (or incense-bearer), carrying the censer with burning **incense**

- **crucifer** (Latin, "cross-bearer"), carrying the processional cross
- **candle-bearers**, each bearing a processional candle, one flanking each side of the cross
- **choir**
- **reader**(s), the person(s) who will read the lessons. This person may carry a large book of Gospels, holding it with the cover facing forward.
- **special Eucharistic ministers**
- **deacon**
- **clergy**
- **celebrant**
- **bishop** (if present)

Sprinkling Rite (Roman). (Latin, *asperges*, "to sprinkle.") The cleansing ceremony in which the **altar** and **congregation** are sprinkled with holy water before the Mass on Sundays, recalling David's words from Psalm 51:2: "Wash away all my iniquity, and cleanse me from my sin." The utensil used for this ceremony is called an **aspergillum**.

Collect for Purity (Anglican). Like the penitential rite in the Roman church, the Collect for Purity is a prayer of preparation for worship. (In the Anglican church, the confession is said right before the Liturgy of the Eucharist.)

> *Almighty God, to you all hearts are open, all desires known, and from you no secrets are hid: Cleanse the thoughts of our hearts by the inspiration of your Holy Spirit, that we may perfectly love you, and worthily magnify your holy Name; through Christ our Lord. Amen.*[32]

confession. The acknowledgment of sin before God. In liturgical worship, part of the penitential rites in which the congregation prays a general confession in preparation for worship. This may also be called *confiteor* (Latin, "I confess").

absolution. The act of absolving sins, pronounced by a priest after confession. In the Eucharist, absolution is a benediction given by the priest following the **confession** of the congregation.

The Ten Commandments or **The Summary of the Law** may be recited. Below is the Summary of the Law:

> *Jesus said, "The first commandment is this: Hear, O Israel: The Lord our God is the only Lord. Love the Lord your God with all your heart, with all your soul, with all your mind, and with all your strength. The second is this: Love your neighbor as yourself. There is no other commandment greater than these."*[33]

Kyrie eleison. (Greek, "Lord have mercy.") A responsive prayer in the penitential rite known as the Lesser Litany. Sometimes simply called "Kyrie." (Interestingly, this is the only bit of Greek in the liturgy.)

> *...every time we stand at the threshold of holy Mass, in which this mercy is celebrated and comes to us in "bodily" form, we cry out: Kyrie, eleison. It is not an accident that the same cry is repeated at the breaking of the bread just before communion: "Lamb of God, you take away the sins of the world; have mercy on us."* (Balthasar Fischer)[34]

Trisagion. Fifth-century liturgical refrain:
> Holy God,
> Holy and Mighty,
> Holy Immortal One,
> Have mercy upon us.[35]

Gloria in excelsis. (Latin, "Glory in the highest.") Sometimes simply called the *Gloria*, a **hymn** containing the angels' song to the Bethlehem shepherds (Luke 2:13–14), sung as part of the entrance rites except in **Advent** and **Lent**. Also called the *Greater Doxology*.

> Glory to God in the highest,
>> and peace to his people on earth.
>
> Lord God, heavenly King,
> almighty God and Father,
>> we worship you, we give you thanks,
>> we praise you for your glory.
>
> Lord Jesus Christ, only Son of the Father,
> Lord God, Lamb of God,
> you take away the sin of the world:
>> have mercy on us;
>
> you are seated at the right hand of the Father:
>> receive our prayer.
>
> For you alone are the Holy One,
> you alone are the Lord,
> you alone are the Most High,
>> Jesus Christ,
>> with the Holy Spirit,
>> in the glory of God the Father. Amen.[36]

The Gloria can also teach us something extremely important: the power that resides in the self-forgetful praise of God the Father and of Christ. Nowhere else in our liturgy does this element of praise emerge so effectively as in the verse from the first part of the Gloria . . . that runs: "We worship you, we give you thanks, we praise you for your glory."

Our prayer is liberating when, like this sentence in the Gloria, it constantly turns into self-forgetful, loving praise of God. It is as though we had sailed from the stifling air of the

*harbor into the refreshing breeze of the open sea; as though
we climbed from the sultry valleys to the heights and the
sharp, strong air that blows there.* (Balthasar Fischer)[37]

Opening Prayer or **Collect of the Day.** A brief formal prayer,
generally connected to the **Epistle** and **Gospel** appointed to the
day, or in some other way appropriate to the day. The collect is
part of the **Propers**.

LITURGY OF THE WORD

lessons. Appointed Scripture passages read at services. There
may be Old Testament, Epistle, and Gospel lessons. Lessons may
also be called *readings*. Each lesson may be followed by a **psalm**,
a **hymn**, or an **anthem**. The lessons and psalm appointed for the
day are found in the **lectionary**.

Psalms. The Old Testament contains 150 psalms or hymns,
which were originally intended to be read or sung **antiphonally**.
A psalm is read or sung after a lesson, followed by the singing of
the *Gloria Patri*. The practice of singing psalms is called
psalmody.

*What is more pleasing than a psalm? David himself puts it
nicely: "Praise the Lord," he says, "for a psalm is good"
(Psalm 146:1). And indeed! A psalm is the blessing of the
people, the praise of God, the commendation of the multi-
tude, the applause of all, the speech of every person, the voice
of the church, the sonorous profession of faith, devotion full
of authority, the joy of liberty, the noise of good cheer, and the
echo of gladness. It softens anger, it gives release from anxiety,
it alleviates sorrow; it is protection at night, instruction by
day, a shield in time of fear, a feast of holiness, the image of
tranquillity, a pledge of peace and harmony, which produces*

*one song from various and sundry voices in the manner of a
cithara. The day's dawning resounds with a psalm, with a
psalm its passing echoes.* (Ambrose)[38]

Gradual. (From Latin, *gradus*, "step," referring to the steps of the
chancel from which the Gradual is sung.) Originally, verses from
the Psalms sung between the first lesson and the **Alleluia** or tract.
Today, this has been replaced by a responsorial psalm or, in some
churches, a **hymn**.

Alleluia. See above, **Liturgical Responses**.

Gospel procession. Before the reading of the Gospel, during
the singing of the hymn, the Bible or **missal** may be moved by
procession to the place from which the Gospel will be proclaimed:
from the Epistle side of the church to the Gospel side; from the
lectern to the center of the church; or from the lectern to the
ambo. This may be a very elaborate procession, complete with
acolytes and **candles**, or a very simple transfer of the book.

Gloria tibi. See above, **Liturgical Responses**.

Gospel. (Anglo-Saxon, "good tidings.") Specifically, the good
news concerning Jesus Christ and salvation in him, found in the
four biographical books of the New Testament which recount his
life and works (Matthew, Mark, Luke, and John). The Gospel lesson
is a passage from one of these books, highlighting a specific event
or teaching from the life of Jesus Christ. The Gospel lesson is one
of the Propers assigned to the day.

Laus tibi. See above, **Liturgical Responses**.

sermon. (Latin, "speech.") A discourse based on a portion of
Scripture, usually one of the appointed lessons, for the purpose of

instructing the congregation in God's will and purpose for **redemption**, a public witness of the **preacher's** and the Christian faith. Sometimes called a *homily* or an *exhortation*.

PROFESSION OF FAITH (THE CREED)

See **chapter 10, We Believe…**

PRAYERS

General Intercessions or **Prayer of the Faithful** or **Prayers of the People**. See above, **Prayers of the People**. In the Anglican tradition, the **Confession of Sin** follows the Prayers of the People.

THE PEACE

The *Pax*. (Latin, "peace.") The **benediction**, "The peace of the Lord be always with you." Also called the *kiss of peace*. The exchange of greeting in the name of the Lord with those gathered for the Eucharist.

> Celebrant: The peace of the Lord be always with you.
> Response: And also with you.

> *Then the deacon cries aloud, "Receive ye one another; and let us kiss one another." Think not that this kiss ranks with those given in public by common friends. It is not such: This kiss blends souls one with another, and solicits for them entire forgiveness. Therefore this kiss is the sign that our souls are mingled together, and have banished all remembrance of wrongs. . . . The kiss therefore is reconciliation, and for this reason holy; as the blessed Paul has in his epistles urged: "Greet ye one another with a holy kiss"; and Peter, "with a kiss of charity." (Cyril of Jerusalem)*[39]

LITURGY OF THE EUCHARIST OR HOLY COMMUNION

Offering. The material gifts of the congregation presented to God at the altar during the service of worship. **Offering plates** of wood or metal are used for conveying the offering to the sanctuary.

- **alms.** (Greek, "mercy.") An offering for the poor, or gifts at any service.
- **oblations.** The gifts presented for use in the liturgy (bread and wine) or, in accordance with ancient custom, for distribution to the poor and sick (food, clothing, etc.).
- **tithe.** The portion of one's income set aside for the church. This may be any percentage, but is often a tenth (Mal. 3:10).

Preparation of the Altar and the Gifts or **the Offertory.**
A transition between the Liturgy of the Word and the Liturgy of the Eucharist, during which lay representatives of the congregation bring to the officiating clergy the **bread box** and the **cruets of wine** and water together with the **offering plates**. (This is considered a procession and is called *Presentation of the Gifts*). The word "Offertory" is also used for the hymn or verses from the Psalms that are sung as the offering is received and while the elements for Communion are being prepared.

doxology. See above, **Liturgical Responses.**

lavabo. (Latin, "I will wash.") The first words of the prayer said as part of the preparations for Eucharist, in which the celebrant washes his fingers in a small basin, while praying silently, "LORD, wash away my iniquity; cleanse me from my sin" (from Ps. 51:2) or Psalm 26:6–12, which begins, "I wash my hands in innocence, and go around your altar, O LORD." The **paten** and the **chalice** are then prepared by the celebrant and his or her assistants before all the people.

EUCHARIST

Eucharistic Prayer. The principal prayer of the Eucharistic liturgy, from opening **dialogue** through the final doxology. Known as the **Great Thanksgiving** in the Anglican rite. Also known as the *anaphora.*

Dialogue. The dialogue at the beginning of the Eucharist that begins with the celebrant's exhortation, "Lift up your hearts." Also known as the *Sursum Corda.* This part of the Eucharist, with the **Preface** and **Sanctus**, gathers all worshipers together "with the angels and archangels and the company of heaven" to join in praise to God.

Preface. One of the most ancient parts of the liturgy, the Preface is the beginning of the Communion Office Propers. Both the Roman and Anglican churches have specific prefaces assigned to each Sunday.

Sanctus (sáhnk-toos). (Latin, "Holy.") The "Hymn of sheer and timeless adoration to the holiness and glory of God" (quoting Massey Shepherd). The *Sanctus* is taken from Isaiah 6:3 (see also Matt. 21:9; Rev. 4:8).

> Holy, holy, holy Lord, God of power and might,
> heaven and earth are full of your glory.
> > Hosanna in the highest.
> Blessed is he who comes in the name of the Lord.
> > Hosanna in the highest.

hosanna. (Hebrew, "save now.") The shout of the throng on **Palm Sunday** (Matt. 21:9, 15; Mark 11:9–10; John 12:13) that now forms the conclusion of the *Sanctus.*

words of institution. The *Verba*. The words used in the celebration of the Eucharist that recall the words of Jesus Christ over the bread and the wine at his Last Supper. It was at this Passover meal with his disciples that Jesus "instituted" this memorial to his sacrificial death (Matt. 26:26–29; Mark 14:22–25; Luke 22:15–20; 1 Cor. 11:23–25).

consecration. As the celebrant recites the words of Jesus Christ (in the words of institution) over the bread and the wine, each is consecrated. In the Roman rite, this is the point at which the bread and wine are changed into the body and blood of Jesus Christ. (In many churches the **Sanctus bells** are rung at the words of consecration.)

elevation. When the words of institution are said, the elements are actually lifted up from the altar and held before the **congregation**.

THE LORD'S PRAYER (SEE ABOVE)

PRAYERS OF THE PEOPLE

Agnus Dei. (Latin, "Lamb of God.") The name of the portion of the Communion service sung just before the **administration**. The words include a portion adapted from John the Baptist when he pointed out Jesus to his disciples in John 1:29: "Look, the Lamb of God, who takes away the sin of the world!"

administration. The giving of the elements to the **communicants** in **Holy Communion**. (Also used to describe the application of the water in the sacrament of **baptism**.) See below for information on receiving **Holy Communion**.

ablution. The ceremonial washing of the **paten, chalice,** and fingers after the **Holy Communion**. This is done by the **celebrant**.

CONCLUDING RITES

recessional. The departure of the **choir** and **clergy** at the conclusion of a service, to the music of a recessional **hymn**.

benediction. A blessing pronounced by the **priest** or **minister** upon the **congregation** at the close of the service. Sources include Numbers 6:24–26; 2 Corinthians 13:14; and Hebrews 13:20–21.

postlude. Organ music played at the close of the service while the worshipers leave the church.

SOME RUBRICS ON RECEIVING HOLY COMMUNION

There have been great theological debates over the centuries about the proper way to receive **Holy Communion**, and today what is deemed correct seems not so much a function of dogma as it is of local custom. While many no doubt will argue differently, the adage "When in Rome . . ." may well have come from trying to answer just such a question. Worship customs vary from church to church, even within the same rite and community, so the best thing to do is watch the locals and do what they do, insofar as possible.

Some churches serve **Holy Communion** using only one **element**, the **bread**. The procedure in these churches is as follows:
- the **communicant** stands or kneels before the **priest**;
- the **bread** is placed on the communicant's tongue by the priest;
- the communicant then returns to his or her place.

Or . . .

- the **communicant** stands or kneels before the **priest** and presents his or her hands cupped together, left hand over right;
- the **bread** is placed in the communicant's hand by the priest;
- using the right hand, the communicant picks up the bread and consumes it;
- the communicant then returns to his or her place and continues in an attitude of **prayer** until all have been served.

Some churches administer both **elements** of **Holy Communion**, that is, both **bread** and **wine**. The procedure in these churches is as follows:
- the **communicant** stands or kneels before the **priest** and presents his or her hands cupped together, left hand over right;
- the **bread** is placed in the communicant's hand by the priest;
- the communicant may carry the bread to the Eucharistic minister or server and dip it into the **wine** and then consume both wine and bread together (**intinction**);
- or, the communicant may consume the bread immediately, then proceed to the chalice, and take a sip of wine (**common cup**). The communicant should help the server guide the chalice;
- the communicant then returns to his or her place and continues in an attitude of **prayer** until all have been served.

Other churches have different traditions: Some process forward to the altar to receive communion, but the wine is served in individual cups that are left at the altar rail in a special holder. In some churches, the people remain in their seats and the **elements** are distributed by the **ushers**. In these churches, everyone waits until all have been served before consuming the bread and the wine at the pastor's word. Again, the best guide is watching the customs of the individual community.

TO KNEEL OR NOT

Kneeling at an **altar rail** is a relatively recent development in church practice. Many churches, especially very old churches and very new churches, do not have altar rails, and Communion is received by standing before the **priest** and/or the Eucharistic minister or server. Whether the people receive kneeling or **standing**, **ushers** direct the movement of people though the process of **Holy Communion**. And again, observing the customs of the church provides the best guide.

UNLIMITED ACCESS

If for some reason it is not possible for a **communicant** to navigate to the **priest**, the priest will come to the communicant where he or she sits in the **nave**. This can be arranged by speaking to a **priest**, a Eucharistic minister, or an **usher**. And if for physical reasons kneeling is difficult, a communicant may stand at the **altar rail**, even though others kneel.

OPEN COMMUNION VERSUS CLOSED COMMUNION

Different churches have different policies about who may receive Communion. In a church that practices closed communion, only those who have been baptized into that specific church tradition may receive communion. Eastern Orthodox churches and Roman Catholic churches, for example, have a closed communion. Other churches offer communion to all who have been baptized, no matter what church performed the baptism. The Anglican church and many **Protestant** churches offer an open communion. Very often who is welcome at the communion table will be indicated by a statement made by the **celebrant** or else noted in the service bulletin.

The paschal mystery is not a cold and lifeless representation of the events of the past, or a simple and bare record of a former age. It is rather Christ himself who is ever living in his church. Here he continues that journey of immense mercy which he began in his mortal life . . . with the design of bringing people to know his mysteries and in a way live by them. These mysteries are ever present and active.
(Mediator Dei)[40]

SIX

The Music of Worship

Sing joyfully to the LORD, you righteous;
it is fitting for the upright to praise him.

Praise the LORD with the harp;
make music to him on the ten-stringed lyre.

Sing to him a new song;
play skillfully, and shout for joy.

For the word of the LORD is right and true;
he is faithful in all he does.

The LORD loves righteousness and justice;
the earth is full of his unfailing love.
(Ps. 33:1–5)

Liturgical music must be like John the Baptist: always pointing
to Christ, never calling attention to itself.
(Brother Roger of Taizé)[41]

THE VOICE OF THE EARLY CHURCH

And you have all been formed into one choir, to . . . sing
God's song together and praise the Father with one voice
through Jesus Christ, that when he hears you he may realize
from what you have done so well that you are of his Son's
members. (Ignatius of Antioch)[42]

The Church has its roots deep in Jewish worship, and the music
of Christian worship grew out of the music of Jewish worship,

resplendent with psalms and **hymns** from the Scriptures. Paul encourages the Ephesians to ". . . be filled with the Spirit. Speak to one another with psalms, hymns and spiritual songs. Sing and make music in your heart to the Lord, always giving thanks to God the Father for everything, in the name of our Lord Jesus Christ" (Eph. 5:18–20). Among the oldest sacred song forms still used in the church today are psalms and **canticles**, the music from the Scriptures.

canticle. (Latin, "little song.") A sacred song or prayer (other than one of the psalms) from the Bible used in liturgical worship, particularly in the **Divine Office** (in the Roman tradition). Old Testament canticles include the two Canticles of Moses (Exod. 15:1–18 and Deut. 32:1–43); the Canticle of Habakkuk (Hab. 3:2–19); the Canticle of Isaiah (Isa. 12:2–6); the Canticle of Hezekiah (Isa. 38:10–20); and the Canticle of Hannah (1 Sam. 2:1–10). The three major New Testament canticles, *Benedictus*, *Nunc Dimittis*, and *Magnificat* (or the "evangelical canticles"), are all taken from the Gospel of Luke. Other familiar canticles include the *Te Deum*, the *Venite* (Psalm 95), and the **Athanasian Creed** (see **chapter 10, We Believe...**).

Benedictus. (Latin, "blessed.") A canticle beginning "Blessed be the Lord, the God of Israel," or in Latin, *Benedictus Dominus Deus*. This is sometimes called the *Song* (or *Canticle*) *of Zechariah*, for these are the words of Zechariah, the father of John the Baptist, found in Luke 1:68–79. It is still sung daily as part of **Matins**.

> Blessed be the Lord, the God of Israel;
>> he has come to his people and set them free.
> He has raised up for us a mighty savior,
>> born of the house of his servant David.
> Through his holy prophets he promised of old,
> that he would save us from our enemies,

from the hands of all who hate us.
He promised to show mercy to our fathers
    and to remember his holy covenant.
This was the oath he swore to our father Abraham,
    to set us free from the hands of our enemies,
Free to worship him without fear,
    holy and righteous in his sight
    all the days of our life.
You, my child, shall be called the prophet of the Most High,
    for you will go before the Lord to prepare his way,
To give his people knowledge of salvation
    by the forgiveness of their sins.
In the tender compassion of our God
    the dawn from on high shall break upon us,
To shine on those who dwell in darkness and the
shadow of death,
    and to guide our feet into the way of peace.[43]

Magnificat. (Latin, "magnify.") A major canticle beginning *Magnificat anima mea Dominum* or "My soul magnifies the Lord." The words are those of the Virgin Mary to Elizabeth found in Luke 1:46–55. This canticle, which is sometimes called the *Song (or Canticle) of Mary*, is sung daily in **Vespers**.

My soul proclaims the greatness of the Lord,
my spirit rejoices in God my Savior;
    for he has looked with favor on his lowly
    servant.
From this day all generations will call me blessed:
    the Almighty has done great things for me,
    and holy is his Name.
He has mercy on those who fear him
    in every generation.
He has shown the strength of his arm,

he has scattered the proud in their conceit.
He has cast down the mighty from their thrones,
and has lifted up the lowly.
He has filled the hungry with good things,
and the rich he has sent away empty.
He has come to the help of his servant Israel,
for he has remembered his promise of mercy,
The promise he made to our fathers,
to Abraham and his children for ever.[44]

Nunc dimittis. (Latin, "Now, you are dismissing [your servant].")
The words are those of Simeon at the **Presentation of Our Lord**
Jesus at the Temple found in Luke 2:29–32. Sometimes called the
Song (or *Canticle*) *of Simeon*, this canticle is sung daily in **Vespers**
in the East and at **Compline** in the West, or during **Evening
Prayer** and **Compline** in the Anglican Church.

Lord, you now have set your servant free
to go in peace as you have promised;
For these eyes of mine have seen the Savior,
whom you have prepared for all the world to see:
A Light to enlighten the nations,
and the glory of your people Israel.[45]

Te Deum (or *Te deum laudamus*). (Latin, "You, God" or more
completely, "We praise you, God.") An ancient canticle of praise,
dating from the fourth century, once attributed to Ambrose of
Milan and Augustine of Hippo, but now considered to be the
composition of Nicetas of Remesiana. The name is taken from the
opening words in Latin.

You are God: we praise you;
You are the Lord: we acclaim you;
You are the eternal Father:
All creation worships you.
To you all angels, all the powers of heaven,

Cherubim and Seraphim, sing in endless praise:
 Holy, holy, holy Lord, God of power and might,
 heaven and earth are full of your glory.
The glorious company of apostles praise you.
The noble fellowship of prophets praise you.
The white-robed army of martyrs praise you.
Throughout the world the holy Church acclaims you;
 Father, of majesty unbounded,
 your true and only Son, worthy of all worship,
 and the Holy Spirit, advocate and guide.
You, Christ, are the king of glory,
the eternal Son of the Father.
When you became man to set us free
you did not shun the Virgin's womb.
You overcame the sting of death
and opened the kingdom of heaven to all believers.
You are seated at God's right hand in glory.
We believe that you will come and be our judge.
 Come then, Lord, and help your people,
 bought with the price of your own blood,
 and bring us with your saints
 to glory everlasting.[46]

Venite. (Latin, "O come.") A canticle beginning with *Venite exultemus* in Latin. An invitation to worship sung at the first canonical hour of the day, **Matins.** The words are from Psalm 95:1–7. Sometimes called the *Invitatory* (Latin, "invitation to adore").
 Come, let us sing to the Lord;
  let us shout for joy to the Rock of our salvation.
 Let us come before his presence with thanksgiving
  and raise a loud shout to him with psalms.

 For the Lord is a great God,
  and a great King above all gods.

In his hand are the caverns of the earth,
   and the heights of the hills are his also.
The sea is his, for he made it,
   and his hands have molded the dry land.

Come, let us bow down, and bend the knee,
   and kneel before the Lord our Maker.
For he is our God,
and we are the people of his pasture and the sheep of his hand.
   Oh, that today you would hearken to his voice![47]

THE VOICES OF THE MONASTERIES

A musical performance also softens hard hearts, leads in the humor of reconciliation, and summons the Holy Spirit. (Hildegard of Bingen)[48]

By the late fourth century, the liturgy of the church had developed into distinct families of Eastern (Greek) and Western (Latin) traditions. The various rites (such as Ambrosian, Gallican, Mozarabic, Gregorian, and Old Roman) developed regionally, creating distinct differences both musically and liturgically. In the eighth century, pressures for political unification under Charlemagne led to liturgical unification as well, and all the local Latin rites except the Ambrosian were suppressed in favor of the Gregorian rite. The Gregorian rite was embraced by the monastic community, where it flowered into the profound body of praises to God that we know as **Gregorian chant**. It was during this time of medieval praise and worship that dedicated **monks** and **nuns** created the first system of musical notation. **Chant** became the music of the time.

antiphon. A response sung in connection with the **antiphonal** reading (or singing) of a psalm or **canticle**.

146

antiphonal. (Greek, "voice against.") Singing responsively on alternate verses of a psalm or **canticle**, usually between two choirs.

chant. Monophonic music in which the text is repeated often and usually sung *a cappella*. Chant is used in worship liturgies, particularly Christian worship, which has its roots in Jewish worship. The most familiar Christian chants may be **Gregorian**.

choral. The plain song of the Roman Catholic Church.

Gregorian chant. (Also called *Plain Chant* or *Plain Song*.) Psalms and canticles chanted on eight tones with dignity and in unison, with the text determining the rhythm. Named after Gregory the Great (seventh century) who wrote a collection of chants called "Antiphonar" and lent his name to the Latin rite that would later become the rite celebrated in most of Western Europe.

intone. To recite on one note. A pastor may intone a service by chanting the parts of the liturgy that would ordinarily be spoken.

monophonic. Music with a single melodic line.

polyphonic. Music that combines two contrasting melodies at one time.

responsorial. Music in which solo singing is joined by the congregation in the refrain.

MUSIC OF THE REFORMATION

In truth we know by experience that song has great force and vigour to move and inflame the hearts of men to invoke and praise God with a more vehement and ardent zeal. (John Calvin)[49]

147

A significant feature of the Reformation was the increase in the availability of Scripture and spiritual knowledge among the laity. What was once the province of clergy now became available to the **congregation**. This was no less true in the realm of church music. Martin Luther, who was instrumental in restoring hymn-singing to the congregation, affirmed, "I place music next to theology and give it the highest praise." The years following the Reformation were rich in the creation of Christian music, by composers such as Georg Frederick Handel, Johann Sebastian Bach, and Felix Mendelssohn, and hymn-writers such as Charles Wesley, John Newton, and Isaac Watts.

anthem. A musical setting of a sacred poem or scripture sung by the **choir** at a stated time in the service.

carol. A joyful **hymn**, particularly a Christmas hymn.

chorale. Harmonized **hymn** tune of the **Protestant** Church introduced by Martin Luther. The most outstanding arranger of chorales was Johann Sebastian Bach.

chorus. Short, energetic song or refrain.

Gospel music. A uniquely American form of Christian music with roots in the rural South. A blend of intricate harmonies, energizing rhythms, and blues-y sound, Gospel music is a tradition in both the African American church and the white rural church.

hymn. A Christian song in **stanza** form sung by the **congregation** at worship.

hymnal. A book containing hymns and the orders of service for worship.

hymnody. The singing or composition of hymns or the great body of hymns available.

praise music. Worship music arising out of the charismatic movement that celebrates especially the activity of the **Holy Spirit** in the lives of Christians.

stanza. Refers to the grouping of the lines of poetry of a hymn. Each stanza requires one playing of the hymn tune.

verse. Each line in the stanza of a hymn.

> *I am not satisfied with those who despise music, as all fanatics do; for music is an endowment and a gift of God, not a gift of other persons. It also drives away the devil and makes people cheerful; one forgets all anger, unchasteness, pride, and other vices. I place music next to theology and give it the highest praise.* (Martin Luther)[50]

SEVEN

The Sacraments

When God took on flesh in Jesus Christ, the uncreated and the created, the eternal and the temporal, the divine and the human, became united. This unity meant that all that is mortal now points to the immortal, all that is finite now points to the infinite. In and through Jesus all creation has become like a splendid veil, through which the face of God is revealed to us.

This is called the sacramental quality of the created order. All that is is sacred because all that is speaks of God's redeeming love. Seas and winds, mountains and trees, sun, moon, and stars, and all the animals and people have become sacred windows offering us glimpses of God.
(Henri Nouwen)[51]

In ancient times, a sacrament (or *sacramentum*, in Latin) was an oath of allegiance to the emperor, evidenced by a branding on the soldier's arm or forehead. The word *sacramentum* was first introduced into Christian vocabulary by Tertullian (third century) who spoke of **Baptism** as a consecration through word (oath) and visible sign (brand) made possible through the Paschal Mystery of Christ, or his **incarnation**, death, and **resurrection**.

The Latin Vulgate later translated the Greek word *mystery* using the word *sacramentum*. *Mystery* is used in the New Testament to described God's hidden plan manifested throughout human history, now made accessible through the **Holy Spirit** to those who have **faith** (Matt. 13:11; Rom. 16:25–26; Eph. 3:4–5). This word was applied to **doctrine** and facts, and only later was it used in reference to rites and practices.

Early Christians regarded **Baptism** and the **Lord's Supper** as rites that expressed both faith and obedience toward God (Matt. 28:19–20; Acts 2:38; Rom. 6:3–5; 1 Cor. 11:23–27; Col. 2:11–12). They are visible representations of **redemption**: Christ lived, died, was raised from the dead, ascended to heaven, and will someday return. Augustine further expanded the connection between mystery and *sacramentum*, so that the rites that memorialize the mystery of redemption came to be known as sacraments. He described a sacrament as a sacred sign or "visible word," composed both of word and physical elements. Sacrament is later defined in **The Book of Common Prayer** as "an outward and visible sign of an inward and spiritual grace."

The sacraments expanded from **Baptism** and the Lord's Supper to include as many as thirty sacraments by the twelfth century, but Thomas Aquinas and later the Council of Trent affirmed only seven sacraments. The Reformation would further define and distill the meaning of sacrament for **Protestants**.

Virtually all Christians recognize **Baptism** and **Eucharist** as sacraments instituted by Christ, by example and by decree (Matt. 3:13–17 and Matt. 26:26–30), though some nonliturgical churches for theological reasons prefer instead to use the term "ordinance." The Roman Catholic Church observes five additional sacraments: **Confirmation**, **Reconciliation** (or penance), **Holy Orders** (ordination), **Marriage** (matrimony), and **Anointing of the Sick** (unction).

BAPTISM

For baptism signifies that the old one and the sinful birth of flesh and blood are to be wholly drowned by the grace of God. We should therefore do justice to its meaning and make baptism a true and complete sign of the thing it signifies.
(Martin Luther)[52]

baptism. (From the Greek, "to dip, to immerse.") One of two great sacraments ordained by Jesus Christ in which water is applied to a person "In the name of the Father, and of the Son, and of the Holy Spirit" (Matt. 28:19), thus admitting the baptized one into the Body of Christ, the Church.

 baptismal shell. It may be a real shell or a shallow metal dish shaped like a shell to hold water for baptism.

believer's baptism. The sacrament offered by those churches that affirm that baptism is available only to those who have made a profession of faith in Jesus Christ. In these churches, it is this profession that admits a believer into the Church, and baptism is the subsequent public seal of that profession.

chrism. (Greek, "an anointing.") A consecrated oil, usually a mixture of olive oil and balsam, used in the administration of baptism. The chrism is applied in the sign of the cross on the baptized person's forehead, as a seal of the covenant of baptism, signifying that this person is "marked as Christ's own forever."

christening. Another term for baptism, particularly of infants and children, that emphasizes becoming a member of God's family and being given a name that is proclaimed to the entire community. Churches that do not practice infant baptism often have a similar service for infants, which they call a *dedication*. This is the commitment of the child to God by its parents, who promise to bring up the child in the faith and offer the child to the service of God (see 1 Sam. 1:27–28).

ewer. A pitcher-like vessel in which the water for baptism is brought to the font.

godparents. At baptism, the witnesses or *sponsors* for the child, who promise to bring him up in the Christian faith that they themselves confess. The parents may be the sponsors or they may appoint others to stand in for them.

shell, with three drops of water. Symbolic of the vessel (the shell) often used to administer baptism. The three drops of water are symbolic of the **Holy Trinity** into which Christians are baptized.

FORMS OF BAPTISM

affusion. Water is poured or sprinkled on the head of the person being baptized as the blessing is pronounced. A font is used for this form of baptism.

immersion. The one being baptized stands in the water with part of the body submerged in water (usually to the waist). Water is then poured over the rest of the body as the blessing is pronounced.

submersion. The candidate is totally covered by the water of baptism, laid backwards into the water while being supported by the officiate. Some traditions call for a single submersion, some for three. Submersion is reminiscent of death to old life and **resurrection** into new life in Christ (Rom. 6:4; Col. 2:12). (This form is often called "immersion" in **Protestant** denominations that practice this form of baptism.) A tank or pool is sometimes provided in the church for this purpose, though some churches prefer to use a natural body of water.

HOLY EUCHARIST

Consider how great is the honor you have been granted; consider how awesome is the table you enjoy. What even angels cannot see without trembling, what they dare not look upon because of its shimmering brightness—that we are fed by; that we are joined to, making us one body and one flesh with Christ.

153

*Through these mysteries, Christ joins himself to each one
of the faithful. Those he begets [in baptism], he nourishes
with his own bodily being . . . proving to you once more that
he has taken on your very flesh. Let us not grow blasé about
being counted worthy of so much love and honor.*
(John Chrysostom)[53]

The word **Eucharist** is Greek for "thanksgiving." The
sacrament instituted by Jesus Christ at his Last Supper with
his disciples, where he commanded them to "Do this in remembrance of me" (Luke 22:14–23; see also Matt. 26:26–29; Mark
14:22–25). Also called the *Lord's Supper*, the *Lord's Table*, the
Blessed Sacrament, *Divine Liturgy*, the *Mass*, and the *Great
Offering*, or *Holy Communion*.

Holy Communion. In the strictest sense, the part of the
Eucharistic service in which the **bread** and **wine** are administered
to the worshipers and they partake of the Lord's body and blood.
"Communion" is the word that the Apostle Paul uses (in the King
James Version) to describe a Christian's interaction with the **elements** of **bread** and **wine**: "The cup of blessing which we bless, is it
not the communion of the blood of Christ? The bread which we
break, is it not the communion of the body of Christ?" (1 Cor.
10:16). Modern translations render this "sharing" or "participation."

element. The **bread** and **wine** used in the **Holy Communion** and
the **water** used in baptism. May also be called *species*.

bread. One of the elements of Holy Communion commanded
to be used by our Lord. In many churches it is used in the form
of an unleavened wafer. This is sometimes called the *host*,
unleavened bread, or *wafer*. The bread used in the Eucharist may
be leavened or unleavened, or may instead be a wafer or host.

- **host.** So-called from the Latin *hostia*, meaning "victim." The flat, round disk of consecrated unleavened bread signifying the sacrificed body of Christ at the Holy Communion. Sometimes embossed with IHS or a cross. Also called a *wafer*.
- **unleavened bread.** Bread made without yeast. Reminiscent of the unleavened bread used in the Passover meal, as ordained by God when the Israelites were preparing to flee Egypt (Exod. 12:1–20).

wine. The second element (or *species*) of the Holy Communion. Sometimes this is called the "Cup," echoing Christ's blessing of the cup in his Last Supper, and the blessing of the four cups of wine during the Passover seder.

- **mixed chalice.** The practice of mixing water with the wine in preparation for Eucharist, followed by most liturgical churches. This reminds us of our reconciliation into Christ through the water of Baptism and is reminiscent of the blood and water that flowed from the side of Christ when he was pierced by the spear during his crucifixion.
- **grape juice.** The fruit of the vine. The element used by some Christian denominations in place of wine in the Communion Service.

administration. The giving of the elements to the communicants in Holy Communion. There are four means of administration:

- **intinction.** (Latin, "to dip in.") The act of dipping the bread into the wine to administer both elements at once. This method is sometimes used with the sick.
- **common cup.** The means of administering the Eucharist wine in which communicants sip from a common **chalice.** A **purificator** is used to clean the edge of the chalice between recipients.
- **spoon.** Used largely in Eastern Orthodox and Eastern Rite churches.

- **straw (tube).** Used largely in Eastern Orthodox and Eastern Rite churches.

reservation. Consecrated elements of the **Holy Communion** reserved for the sick. A custom more prevalent in the Roman Catholic Church.

consubstantiation. As generally defined, the body and blood of our Lord are communicated by means of the consecrated elements, which remain bread and wine. The four are in union. This **doctrine** is counter to that of transubstantiation as held by the Roman Catholic Church.

transubstantiation. The **doctrine** of the Roman Catholic Church that in Communion, the substance of the bread and wine are changed into the body and blood of Christ, while the appearances of bread and wine remain.

OTHER SACRAMENTS
CONFIRMATION

A rite administered only to those who have been baptized, in which the **confirmand** (candidate for confirmation) now reaffirms and takes upon himself the baptismal vows and comes into full membership in the church. Confirmation is bestowed by the **imposition of hands** (or the **laying on of hands**) by the officiating clergy (usually the **bishop**) onto the heads of those being confirmed.

> *Almighty and everliving God, let your fatherly hand ever be over these your servants; let your Holy Spirit ever be with them; and so lead them in the knowledge and obedience of your Word, that they may serve you in this life, and dwell with you in the life to come; through Jesus Christ our Lord. Amen. (The Book of Common Prayer)*[54]

ANOINTING OF THE SICK

This sacrament was formerly known as *unction*, and in the case of those near death, *extreme unction* (Latin, "last anointing"). As part of the Church's pastoral care of the sick, anointing with **holy oil** is intended to strengthen anyone whose health has been affected by illness or old age.

chrism or **holy oils**. Those oils that have been consecrated by a **priest** or **bishop** to be used in certain rites of the Church. The chrism is ordinarily made with olive oil and balsam or a perfume oil. A legacy of Jewish worship and practice, anointing with oil has been practiced since the earliest days of the church. Though commonly associated with the sacrament of unction, (the Anointing of the Sick), the chrism may also be used in **ordination** and in initiation rites such as **Baptism**, **Confirmation**, and **Eucharist**. Generally, the bishop consecrates the chrism at a special Chrism Mass celebrated on **Maundy Thursday** morning.

> *As you are outwardly anointed with this holy oil, so may our heavenly Father grant you the inward anointing of the Holy Spirit. Of his great mercy, may he forgive you your sins, release you from suffering, and restore you to wholeness and strength. May he deliver you from all evil, preserve you in all goodness, and bring you to everlasting life; through Jesus Christ our Lord. Amen. (The Book of Common Prayer)*[55]

MARRIAGE

Also called *matrimony*. The rite or ceremony in which a man and a woman establish a lifelong partnership, committing to each other's well-being and to the care of children. All Christians consider the marriage vows sacred, a covenant made before God and before witnesses that echoes the relationship between God and his people and Jesus Christ and his Church.

O God of our Fathers, bless these thy servants, and sow the seed of eternal life in our hearts; that whatsover in thy holy word they shall profitably learn, they may indeed fulfill the same; that so, obeying thy will, and always being in safety under thy protection, they may abide in thy love unto their lives' end; through Jesus Christ our Lord. (The Prayer Book as proposed in 1928 in England)[56]

banns. (Anglo-Saxon, "to proclaim.") The notice of intention of marriage publicly given in the church in which the ceremony will take place.

HOLY ORDERS

Also called *ordination.* The sacrament through which one is received into the **ministry** of the Church as a **deacon**, **priest**, or **bishop**. Ordination means to be set apart for a particular office or duty (Jer. 1:5; Mark 3:14; John 15:16; Acts 6:3, 14:23; 1 Tim. 2:7; Titus 1:5; Heb. 5:1, 8:3). In apostolic times, those ordained for a certain work in the Church were set apart by the **laying on of hands** (Acts 6:6; 1 Tim. 4:14; 2 Tim. 1:6), a rite that is practiced to this day.

charge. An address containing instructions, to **ordinands** at their ordination, or to the **congregation** and the **pastor** at the pastor's **installation**.

laying on of hands or **imposition of hands.** The placing of hands by the officiating clergy on the heads of those being ordained. **Apostolic succession** is maintained through this rite. (See also below, in chapter 8, under **Hands.**)

installation. The service of induction that "sets in the **stall**" the new **pastor** of the **congregation**, or other officers in their positions.

---

ordinand. A candidate for ordination.

RECONCILIATION

The sacrament in which sinners are reconciled to God and to the Church. Modeled after the work and teaching of Jesus, reconciliation acknowledges that sin is an offense against both God and the community. Its goal is the prayerful restoration of these relationships. This sacrament is sometimes known as *penance.*

absolution. (Latin, "to free from.") The declaration of the forgiveness of sins made by the minister on the authority of God to those who have confessed and are repentant (John 20:22–23).

penance. An act of **repentance** for sin, which may be part of the process of reconciliation. A penance may consist of **prayer, fasting,** charity to one's neighbor, good works, or sacramental acts.

> *Reconciliation in the New Testament sense does not consist in plea bargaining with God. Nor does it have anything to do with amassing virtue so that God will somehow be forced, in justice, to bestow grace and salvation. If the radical meaning of repentance is "recognition and response," then the meaning of reconciliation is obedience and surrender. Being obedient to the word of the gospel does not mean the perfect fulfilling of laws, regulations and prescriptions. It means, instead, letting go, giving up our pretentious claims to goodness and holiness, surrendering to the power of God's love that burns even our virtues away.* (Nathan Mitchell)[57]

EIGHT

Private Worship

SPIRITUAL DISCIPLINES

. . . we can become like Christ by doing one thing—by follow-ing him in the overall style of life he chose for himself. If we have faith in Christ, we must believe that he knew how to live. We can, through faith and grace, become like Christ by practicing the types of activities he engaged in, by arranging our whole lives around the activities he himself practiced in order to remain constantly at home in the fellowship of his Father.

What activities did Jesus practice? Such things as solitude and silence, prayer, simple and sacrificial living, intense study and meditation upon God's Word and God's ways, and service to others. Some of these will certainly be even more necessary to us than they were to him, because of our greater or different need. (Dallas Willard)[58]

abstinence. The act of voluntary forbearance for a certain period of time as an act of personal penance. This may involve anything from a special food to sexual relations.

confession. The acknowledgment of sin, either corporately as part of liturgical worship or privately through confessing one's sins to a priest who is authorized to forgive them in the Name of Jesus. In the Roman Catholic Church, confession is part of the sacrament of **Reconciliation.**

fasting. To voluntarily abstain from foods for a specified length of time. A biblical practice observed by Jesus and the early Church, fasting is intended as a spiritual discipline. In the liturgical church, the seasons designated for fasting are **Advent** and **Lent**; Vatican II reforms require fasting only on **Ash Wednesday** and **Good Friday**.

> *At bottom, Christian fasting represents a serious effort to enter into the suffering death of Christ so as to share more fully in his Easter life. The Church does not preach abnegation for the sake of abnegation. In the spring of the year she bids us take a beneficial pruning hook to the tree, not because she wants the sharp cuts to bring pain to the tree, but because this painful action helps the tree blossom and bear fruit.* (Balthasar Fischer)[59]

lectio divina. (Latin, "divine reading.") A spiritual discipline of the reading of Scripture that grew out of the monastic experience. It was formalized by the Rule of St. Benedict of Nursia, which made *lectio* a substantial element in each day's schedule. *Lectio divina* uses the meditative reading of Scripture as a gateway to prayer:

> *Above all, lectio is undertaken in the conviction that God's word is meant to be a "good" word—that is, something carrying God's own life in a way that is beneficial to one who receives it faithfully. Lectio turns to the Scripture in order that we be nourished, comforted, refreshed by it. Lectio is an encounter with the living God. It is prayer.* (Norvene Vest)[60]

meditation. A spiritual discipline in which the mind is focused so as to move deeper into God's presence.

pilgrimage. A journey to visit a place made sacred by its association with a holy person or event. An act of religious devotion, a pilgrimage involves the entire journey: the traveling to and the returning home as well as the visit itself. A pilgrimage is a reminder of the journey that the Christian travels through life. *The Canterbury Tales* are stories from a religious pilgrimage to the cathedral at Canterbury.

prayer. Perhaps the most elemental and significant of all spiritual disciplines, prayer is personal communication with God, through thanksgiving, adoration, petition, and **repentance**. Jesus taught his followers to pray, primarily by example (in the desert, in Gethsemane). When his disciples said, "Lord, teach us to pray" (Luke 11:1), Jesus provided them a concrete example (Luke 11:2–4; Matt. 6:9–13). Perhaps the most important gift Jesus offered his disciples was that they could pray to the Father in the name of Jesus (John 14:13–14; 16:23–24), giving his followers a new standing for entering into the presence of God and being transformed by his Spirit.

> . . . *prayer is nothing more than an ongoing and growing love relationship with God the Father, Son, and Holy Spirit.* (Richard Foster)[61]

retreat. A withdrawal from the world for a period of prayer, **meditation**, study, and spiritual renewal. Retreats may be made alone or with others, and may be as short as a day or two or last as long as a week or more. Some retreats are directed, that is, they follow a plan set out by a spiritual director; retreats may or may not be silent.

POPULAR DEVOTION

Angelus. The Angelus, whose name is taken from the opening words *Angelus Domini nuntiavit Maria* (Latin, "The angel of the Lord declared to Mary . . ."), is a devotion honoring the Incarnation. It consists of praying three introductory and one concluding **versicles** and responses interspersed with three Hail Marys. The distinctive element of this devotion is the bells that call people to prayer. Called appropriately **Angelus bells**, they are rung three times daily, at 6 AM, noon, and 6 PM, in a pattern of three peals rung three times. There may be a longer peal added to the 6 PM ringing.

Hail Mary. (In Latin, *Ave Maria*.) A prayer that uses the words of the angel to Mary at the **Annunciation** (Luke 1:28) and Elizabeth's greeting to Mary at the **Visitation** (Luke 1:42). Part of the **Divine Office** from the sixteenth century and used today as part of the prayers of the **Rosary.**

Hail Mary, full of grace, the Lord is with thee.
Blessed art thou among women, and blessed is the fruit of thy womb, Jesus.
Holy Mary, mother of God, pray for us sinners, now, and at the hour of our death. Amen.

Jesus Prayer. An ancient prayer from the Eastern Church, repeated over and over again as a meditation, with the intention of shutting out distractions and releasing the person praying deeper into the presence of God. This form of meditational prayer is the subject of the classic work *The Way of the Pilgrim*.

"Lord Jesus Christ, Son of God, have mercy on me, a sinner."

novena. (From Latin *novem*, "nine.") A devotion in which specified prayers are repeated nine successive times (for example, nine successive days, nine successive Mondays, etc.). These prayers may be offered for a special intention. Chiefly used in the Roman Catholic Church.

Rosary. A form of counted prayer (specifically Roman Catholic) using a string of beads (called a rosary) consisting of fifteen decades of beads (a decade is ten beads). Each decade is counted while praying the "Hail Mary" at each bead, and is preceded by the Lord's Prayer and completed by the *Gloria Patri*. Each of the fifteen decades is associated with a meditation from the life of Jesus Christ, called a sacred mystery, which recalls events from his birth and early life (Joyful Mysteries), his Passion and death (Sorrowful Mysteries), and his Resurrection and Ascension (Glorious Mysteries). In 2002, Pope John Paul II recommended an additional set of mysteries, called the Luminous Mysteries, which focus on the ministry and teaching of Jesus Christ. Dating from the thirteenth century, the Rosary is a means of focus and deeper meditation on the person of Jesus Christ.

Stations of the Cross or **Way of the Cross.** During the Middle Ages, when pilgrimages to the Holy Land became more common, pilgrims, as an act of devotion, began to trace the route traveled by Jesus as he left the house of Pilate on his journey to Calvary. The Stations of the Cross were developed as a way to bring this pilgrimage into a local church, so that all worshipers could share the experience.

First Station	Jesus is condemned to death
Second Station	Jesus receives the cross
Third Station	Jesus falls the first time
Fourth Station	Jesus is met by his blessed mother
Fifth Station	Simon of Cyrene helps Jesus carry his cross
Sixth Station	Veronica wipes the face of Jesus
Seventh Station	Jesus falls the second time

Eighth Station   The women of Jerusalem weep for our Lord
Ninth Station   Jesus falls the third time
Tenth Station   Jesus is stripped of his garments
Eleventh Station   Jesus is nailed to the cross
Twelfth Station   Jesus dies on the cross
Thirteenth Station   Jesus is taken down from the cross
Fourteenth Station   Jesus is placed in the tomb

OBJECTS OF DEVOTION

A particular toy or a particular icon may be itself a work of art, but that is logically accidental; its artistic merits will not make it a better toy or a better icon. They may make it a worse one. For its purpose is, not to fix attention upon itself, but to stimulate and liberate certain activities in the child or the worshiper. The teddy bear exists in order that the child may endow it with imaginary life and personality and enter into a quasi-social relationship with it. That is what "playing with it" means. The better this activity succeeds the less the actual appearance of the object will matter. Too close or prolonged attention to its changeless and expressionless face impedes the play. A crucifix exists in order to direct the worshiper's thought and affections to the Passion. It had better not have any excellencies, subtleties, or originalities which will fix attention upon itself. Hence devout people may, for this purpose, prefer the crudest and emptiest icon. The emptier, the more permeable; and they want, as it were, to pass through the material image and go beyond. (C. S. Lewis)[62]

Personal worship in the Roman Catholic Church and the Eastern Orthodox Church includes the use of images and **relics**. What may appear as worship to those from other traditions is more accurately *veneration*, which is to show devotion, honor, and respect to God, Jesus Christ, a saint, or an angel, through the use of images or relics, in particular. This show of honor may include prayers, lighting candles (especially **votives**), caresses, kisses, and other gestures of devotion.

The Church is of many minds on the subject of images in worship. God's instructions to the Jews were to use no images at all in their worship. The early Church, with its roots deep in Judaism, apparently shared that belief. But as the Church spread among Gentiles, paintings and images began to decorate first their graves (the catacombs) and later their churches.

The role of images in Christian worship was vigorously debated first in the eighth century by the iconoclasts, who destroyed **icons** and persecuted those who supported their use. Later, Reformation **Protestants** objected to the abuses and misunderstandings involved with images.

To those who use images as an integral part of their devotional life, there is no confusion. Rather, images function like windows, through which a worshiper sees into the eternal, just as Jesus is the image (icon) of God.

icon. A religious image typically painted on a small wooden panel and used in the devotions of Eastern Christians in particular.

relic. An object esteemed and venerated because of its association with a saint or martyr. The container or shrine in which it is kept is called a *reliquary*.

statue. Three-dimensional image of Jesus Christ, Mary, an angel, or a saint. Statues are venerated because they represent particular persons or beings who share God's holiness.

votive candle. A candle in a small glass cup, representing continuing prayer, often for a special intention. Votives may be placed before an icon or another sacred representation, or be displayed with other votives on special tables at various places in the church.

GESTURES AND POSTURES

Those new to the liturgical tradition may be startled by the considerable amount of movement during the service. The uninitiated may perceive no rhyme or reason to the **bowing**, the **standing**, the sitting, and the **kneeling**. Indeed, such movement may appear to have all the mystery of a secret handshake.

Bowing and kneeling have always been a part of human worship as signs of humility and reverence. In Paul's letter to the Philippians (2:9–11), he included the words to an early hymn describing Jesus:

Therefore God exalted him to the highest place
  and gave him the name that is above every name,
that at the name of Jesus every knee should bow,
  in heaven and on earth and under the earth,
and every tongue confess that Jesus Christ is Lord,
  to the glory of God the Father.

It is the words "every knee should bow" that acknowledge the posture that Christians assume before their Lord and Savior. It is this hymn as well that provides the key reason for bowing and kneeling: "at the name of Jesus. . . . " During the liturgy, it is at the name of Jesus that heads bow. And by extension, it is to those things that remind us of him, that worshipers bow or kneel.

To those who come from nonliturgical traditions, bowing and kneeling may seem utterly foreign and even distasteful, enough to keep a person from participating. But all aspects of worship are intended to point the worshiper to Jesus, even things as fundamental as posture. Kneeling recalls the bedtime prayers of childhood and bowing reminds us of the honor ascribed to greatness. Sometimes the body can remember what the mind forgets. And as C. S. Lewis points out, "The body ought to pray as well as the soul. Body and soul are both the better for it."[63]

167

There are no penalties for not bowing at the right places during the liturgy. And the only hazard in not kneeling at the right points in the service is a brief moment of standing alone. But no one wants to feel self-conscious or out of step, so here's a good rule for liturgical situations:

We sit for instruction, we stand for praise, and we kneel to pray.

bowing. An inclination of the head and body, or just the head. Liturgically, bowing is a sign of supplication and adoration toward God; bowing also can indicate respect or reverence toward a person or thing, or express a greeting. In the Roman Church, the head is bowed

- at the doxology (in which the **Holy Trinity** is invoked);
- at the name of Jesus, Mary, or the saint of the day; and
- at the consecration of the Eucharist.

Bowing of the body is made
- before the altar, and
- at specified times during the Mass.

In Anglican churches, people may bow
- as the processional cross passes by;
- before the altar;
- at the Name of Jesus;
- at the mention of the **Holy Trinity**;
- toward the Book of the Gospel at the *Gloria tibi* and the *Laus tibi*;
- during the **creed**, at the words describing the Incarnation (called the *incarnatus*; see **genuflect**).
- A bow also is exchanged between the **thurifer** and those being incensed when incense is used.

genuflect, genuflection, or **genuflexion.** (Latin, "to bend the knee.") The act of recognizing the presence of God in the **Holy Eucharist** by bending the right knee upon entering and leaving the pew while facing the altar. Some also genuflect at the words in the Nicene Creed: "was incarnate of the Holy Spirit and the Virgin Mary and became truly human." These words are called the *Incarnatus* from the Latin for Incarnation.

kneeling. The posture often assumed for private or corporate prayer as an expression of humility before God, reflecting both an attitude of **penance** and an attitude of adoration.

> *On entering a church, or in passing before the altar, kneel down all the way without haste and hurry, putting your heart into what you do, and let your whole attitude say, Thou art the great God. It is an act of humility, an act of truth, and every time you kneel it will do your soul good.* (Romano Guardini)[64]

standing. The posture of respect that worshipers assume for processions, the reading of the Gospel, the creed, and the prayers of the people. It is also used from the **Presentation of the Gifts** through the breaking of the bread, and then at the **Prayer after Communion** and the recessional.

> *Standing is the other side of reverence toward God. Kneeling is the side of worship in rest and quietness; standing is the side of vigilance and action. It is the respect of the servant in attendance, of the soldier on duty.* (Romano Guardini)[65]

HANDS

> *There is greatness and beauty in this language of the hands. The Church tells us that God has given us our hands in order that we may "carry our souls" in them. The Church is fully in earnest in the use she makes of the language of gesture. She speaks her innermost mind, and God gives ear to this mode of speaking.* (Romano Guardini)[66]

169

benediction. A benediction, or blessing, may be conferred by making the **sign of the cross** over the people while saying the words of the benediction, although it may also be offered by simply raising the right hand (palm down) over the people.

laying on of hands (or **imposition of hands**). The hand(s) are placed upon the head or shoulders of the recipient for the following purposes:

- bestowing blessing and benediction (Gen. 48:13–20; Matt. 19:13, 15; cf. Mark 10:16; Luke 24:50);
- healing (e.g., Matt. 9:18; Mark 1:41; Acts 9:12, 17; 28:8);
- reception of the Holy Spirit and spiritual gifts in **baptism** (Acts 8:17, 19; 19:6; 1 Tim. 4:14; 2 Tim. 1:6);
- **ordaining** or commissioning (Acts 6:6; 13:3).

prayer. Traditionally, hands are folded in an attitude of prayer during liturgy, either with fingers intertwined or with palms and fingertips touching. Both indicate an attitude of attention and petition.

sign of the cross. Blessings may be also conferred by making the sign of the cross, which is probably the most familiar gesture seen in the liturgical church. It is used as a way of sanctifying actions in daily life and as an encouragement in difficult times.

When used to bless another, the right hand is raised and the sign of the cross is made over the **congregation**, individual, or object being blessed. Also, the **priest** may bless an individual simply by drawing a cross on the person's forehead with the thumb, as when blessing an infant or child during **Holy Communion** (in lieu of administering Eucharist).

The sign of the cross is also a response of a worshiper during the liturgy to an invocation of the **Holy Trinity**, or at specified points in the Mass (at the beginning of the service, during absolution, during the **creed**, during the Eucharist). Often the **missal** will use a symbol of a cross (such as ✠ or +) within the text when a worshiper should make the sign of the cross.

In the Roman rite, the sequence of the movements is as follows: forehead to breast, left shoulder, right shoulder, center of breast. In the East, the right shoulder is touched before the left. In the West, the hand is open during the sign of the cross. In the East, the hand is held with the thumb and first two fingertips pressed together (representing the **Holy Trinity**) and the last two fingers pressed down to the palm (representing the two natures of Christ, and his coming down to earth).

Before reading the **Gospel**, the priest may first make the sign of the cross on the Gospel page, then draw a cross with the thumb over the forehead, lips, and heart, while saying the following prayer: "May the gospel be in my mind to understand it, on my lips to proclaim it, and in my heart to live it," or "May the Lord purify my understanding, my speech, and my heart, so that I may receive the words of the gospel."

striking the breast. A gesture of penitence, used especially in the pre-Vatican II rite when in the confession the **priest** prays three times the words *"mea culpa"* ("through my fault") while striking his or her breast.

> *To strike the breast is to beat against the gates of our inner world in order to shatter them.* (Romano Guardini)[67]

worship. Increasingly, liturgical churches are seeing worshipers lift their hands in enthusiastic response to worship.

- as an offering to God:
    May my prayer be set before you like incense;
        may the lifting up of my hands be like the evening
        sacrifice (Ps. 141:2);
- lifted high in praise:
    I will praise you as long as I live,
        and in your name I will lift up my hands (Ps. 63:4);
    Lift up your hands in the sanctuary
        and praise the LORD (Ps. 134:2);

- with palms up in supplication:
    Hear my cry for mercy
        as I call to you for help,
    as I lift up my hands
        toward your Most Holy Place
        (Ps. 28:2);
    I spread out my hands to you;
        my soul thirsts for you like a parched land
        (Ps. 143:6);
- clapping:
    Clap your hands, all you nations;
        shout to God with cries of joy (Ps. 47:1);
- in gratitude:
    I lift up my hands to your commands, which I love,
        and I meditate on your decrees (Ps. 119:48).

Silence is not simply the absence of noise or the shutdown of communication with the outside world, but rather a process of coming to stillness. Silent solitude forges true speech. I'm not speaking of physical isolation; solitude here means being alone with the Alone, experiencing the transcendent Other, and growing in awareness of one's identity as the beloved. It is impossible to know another person intimately without spending time together. Silence makes this solitude a reality. It has been said, "Silence is solitude practiced in action."
(Brennan Manning)[68]

NINE

Lessons and Books of Worship

The Jews are known as the "people of the Book," and as their heirs, Christians anchor their own faith to the Book as well. The Bible is the revelation of God, his word given to the Jews as a record of his interaction with and faithfulness to his people. Jesus is God's Word incarnate (John 1:1–5, 14), and it is this Word that reveals God's profound love for his creation.

In the early Church, worship and Scriptures were available in the languages of the worshipers. The translation of the Scriptures into Latin was motivated by the need to offer these important writings in a language that many people of different nations spoke, wrote, and read. As the centuries passed, Latin became the language not of the everyday people but of the educated classes. Everyday folks spoke what would be called today "native languages," but their worship was conducted in Latin, a language understood by few and read by fewer.

The invention of movable-type printing presses precipitated many social changes, not the least of which was the impulse to print the Bible in the languages that people understood and used. In many ways the Reformation was the reassertion of the Word, so it is not surprising that the invention of movable-type printing presses and the rise of using the vernacular in Scriptures and worship coincided.

Books have become essential to our worship, and at the center is of course the Bible, the word of God. From there, we move on to **missals**, prayer books, **breviaries**, **hymnals**, and **catechisms**, all of which serve to guide and enhance our worship experience. As these bound bits of ink and paper lead us day by day into the presence of God, we learn to allow the words to carry us to the place where words do not suffice.

173

BIBLE

The Bible (Greek, *biblia*, "short writings") is the book of sacred writings that have been accepted by Christians as inspired by God (2 Pet. 1:21) and of divine authority, on which the Christian religion is based. May also be called the *Holy Bible* or *Scriptures* or *Holy Scriptures* (Latin, *scriptura*, "act or product of writing").

The canon of the Bible, in **Protestant** traditions, includes 39 books from the Jewish Scriptures (*Tanakh*), which Christians typically know as the Old Testament, and the 27 books of the New Testament. The word *canon* is Greek, meaning "rule," and the canon of the Bible comprises Scriptures that are authoritative and, as such, are the "rule" for faith and life.

The Roman Catholic, Anglican, and Orthodox traditions include in the Bible additional books and material that had been collected with the Jewish Scriptures in the two hundred years before the birth of Jesus. This material was not considered canonical, but still important as informative literature. These writings are called the *Deuterocanon* by the Roman Catholic Church (or the *Apocrypha* by **Protestants**).

The Bible was written by many authors and contains many kinds of literature, which can be generally classified as poetry, law, history, prophecy, apocalyptic writing, Wisdom literature, Gospels, and Epistles. The Old Testament contains the Pentateuch (Torah); history; poetry; Major Prophets; and Minor Prophets. The New Testament is comprised of the Gospels; history; and the Epistles.

The original languages of the Bible were Hebrew and Aramaic for the Jewish portions, and Greek for New Testament books. The history of the English Bible includes the following milestones:

The Vulgate, translated into Latin by Jerome, around AD 390
Douai, 1610 (Rheims New Testament, 1582) (Roman Catholic)
King James Version (KJV), 1611
English Revised Version, 1881
American Standard Version (ASV), 1901
Revised Standard Version (RSV), 1952
New English Bible (NEB), 1961
Jerusalem Bible (JB), 1966 (Roman Catholic)
New American Bible (NAB), 1970 (Roman Catholic)
New Jerusalem Bible (NJB), 1985 (Roman Catholic)
New American Standard Bible (NASB), 1971
The Living Bible (LB), 1971
New International Version (NIV), 1978
New King James Version (NKJV), 1982
New Revised Standard Version (NRSV), 1989
New Living Bible (NLB), 1996
English Standard Version (ESV), 2001
The Message: The Bible in Contemporary Language, 2002
Holman Christian Standard Version (HCSV), 2004
New Living Translation, 2nd edition (NLT), 2004
Today's New International Version (TNIV), 2005

The Bible is organized into individual books, each of which is divided by:

- **chapter**. The numbered divisions of a book of the Bible.
- **verse**. The numbered divisions of a chapter in the Bible.

SYMBOLS OF THE BIBLE

book. In the fourth century, with the development of the codex, the book replaced the scroll as the symbol for learning, writing, and teaching, and by extension, knowledge and wisdom. Symbolizes the Bible (see also **scroll**) and divine authorship. In medieval thought, the closed book represented mystery, the sealed book represented impenetrable secrecy, and the open book represented teaching the truth of the Gospel.

open book, with the words *Spiritus Gladius* (Latin for "the Sword of the Spirit"). Symbolizes Holy Scripture.

open book, with the initials VDMA or the words *Verbum Dei Manet in Aeternum* (Latin for ". . . the word of the Lord stands forever," 1 Pet. 1:25, a quotation taken from Isa. 40:6–8). Symbolizes Holy Scripture.

lamp. Represents the Word of God (Ps. 119:105).

pen or **quill,** with scroll or inkwell (inkhorn). Divine authorship.

scroll. The earliest writings of Scripture were recorded on parchment or papyrus scrolls, so the scroll represents the Word of God, spoken and written, particularly the books of the Old Testament. It also represents the gift of writing when included in the representation of a saint. One scroll may represent the Pentateuch (Torah, the Law) or the entirety of Holy Scriptures. Two Scrolls: Old and New Testaments. Four scrolls: the Four Gospels. Twelve scrolls: the twelve Epistles of St. Paul. May be shown with an author's name written on it.

wings. May be used with a book to represent the spread of the Gospel. Wings also may appear on the symbols of each evangelist for the same purpose. See **St. John** (December 29), **St. Mark** (April 25), **St. Matthew** (September 21), and **St. Luke** (October 18).

PARTICULAR WRITINGS

Beatitudes. The teaching of Jesus about life in his kingdom, from his Sermon on the Mount (Matthew 5–7).

Ten Commandments. The laws given to Moses on Mount Sinai that form the foundation for all God's laws regarding a person's relationship to God and others (Exod. 20:2–17; Deut. 5:6–21). These laws were later affirmed and summarized by Jesus (e.g., Mark 12:29–31). Also called the *Decalogue*, the Ten Commandments are symbolized by tablets of stone with the commandments written on them or with the numbers 1 through 10 in Roman numerals.

THE WORD IN LITURGY

lectionary. A listing of biblical texts to be read as lessons or readings in worship services. The latest revisions of the Roman Catholic lectionary for Sunday Mass, Daily Mass, and the Daily Office have been made since Vatican II. The lectionary for Sunday and the Daily Office found in the Book of Common Prayer (The Episcopal Church/Anglican Communion) is based on the Roman Catholic Lectionary. Recently, the major denominations cooperated to create the Revised Common Lectionary, using the Roman Lectionary as its foundation. Now the Episcopal/Anglican, Lutheran, Methodist, Presbyterian, Reformed, Disciples of Christ, and Roman Catholic Churches and many other churches are quite often reading the same lessons on the same Sundays, with only slight variations, creating a profound link among the various parts of the Body of Christ. By Advent 2010, the Episcopal Church will have officially replaced its current lectionary with the Revised Common Lectionary.

pericope. (Greek, "a section.") The portions of Scripture that are read as the Gospel and Epistle lessons.

psalter. The book containing the psalms sung in the liturgy.

tables. A catalog of lessons, proper hymns, and psalms or feasts of the church year, as they are defined and appear in the liturgical tools of the church.

BOOKS OF WORSHIP

The Book of Common Prayer. The worship book of the Church of England first compiled by Archbishop Thomas Cranmer, who headed a commission charged with creating a single, convenient, and comprehensive book of worship in English, based in part on the Latin services of the medieval Church and including some revisions proposed by **Protestant** Reformers. In 1549, the First Prayer Book of Edward VI was printed, and Parliament passed an act requiring its use. In addition to the orders for services, the current Prayer Book in use in the United States (published in 1979) contains a **catechism**, the **Articles of Religion**, the Psalms, the **lectionary**, and the **Propers**.

breviary. (From Latin, *brevarium*, "an abridgment.") The book containing the lessons, psalms, hymns, etc., used in the **Divine Office** (or the **Liturgy of the Hours**) in the Roman Catholic Church. Sometimes called a *Book of Hours*.

missal or **sacramentary.** (From Latin, *liber missalis*, "book of the Mass.") The altar (Mass) book containing the order of services used in the Roman Catholic Church. The missal contains both the **ordinary** and **Proper** parts of the **Mass**. Prior to the thirteenth century, the parts of the Mass were distributed over a number of separate books to be used by various participants in the liturgy, such as the *Graduale* and *Antiphonale*, used by the choir; the *Apostolus* (letters of the New Testament), used by the **subdeacon**; the *Evangelarium* (Gospel), used by the **deacon**; and the *Sacramentarium*, which contained all the prayers of the Mass and was used by the **celebrant**. In order to accommodate the growing practice of private Mass, these books were gathered into one volume for the **priest**, who celebrated all the parts of the Mass alone.

rubric. (Latin, "red.") The directions for the officiant and participants, so-called because they were originally written (and are now often printed) in the service book in red ink.

INSTRUCTION IN THE FAITH

catechism. A book of instruction explaining the **Ten Commandments**, the **creed**, the **Sacraments**, and the **Lord's Prayer**. It is in a question-and-answer form to be used in teaching the Christian doctrine, especially to those preparing to join the church. Among the more familiar catechisms are the Heidelberg and Geneva catechisms of the Reformed Church; Luther's Larger and Smaller Catechisms (Lutheran Church); the Anglican catechism, called "An Outline of the Christian Faith," found in **The Book of Common Prayer**; and the Roman Catholic catechisms, the Baltimore Catechism (1885), and most recently, *The Catechism of the Catholic Church* (1994).

> *Blessed Lord, who hast caused all Holy Scriptures to be written for our learning: Grant that we may in such wise hear them, read, mark, learn, and inwardly digest them, that by patience, and comfort of thy holy Word, we may embrace, and ever hold fast the blessed hope of everlasting life, which thou has given us in our Saviour Jesus Christ. Amen.*
> *(The Book of Common Prayer, 1549)*[69]

179

TEN

We Believe...

CREEDS

The word *creed* originates from the Latin word *credo*, which means "I believe." A creed is a statement of Christian doctrine confessed by all believers and is included in most liturgical services. A creed is sometimes called a *symbol*, from the Latin *symbolum*. There are three creeds: Apostles', Nicene, and Athanasian.

> . . . *it is worse than useless for Christians to talk about the importance of Christian morality, unless they are prepared to take their stand upon the fundamentals of Christian theology. It is a lie to say that dogma does not matter; it matters enormously. It is fatal to let people suppose that Christianity is only a mode of feeling; it is vitally necessary to insist that it is first and foremost a rational explanation of the universe. It is hopeless to offer Christianity as a vaguely idealistic aspiration of a simple and consoling kind; it is, on the contrary, a hard, tough, exacting, and complex doctrine, steeped in a drastic and uncompromising realism. And it is fatal to imagine that everybody knows quite well what Christianity is and needs only a little encouragement to practice it. The brutal fact is that in this Christian country not one person in a hundred has the faintest notion what the Church teaches about God or man or society or the person of Jesus Christ.*
> (Dorothy L. Sayers)[70]

THE APOSTLES' CREED

A statement of **faith** summarizing the **doctrines** taught by the Apostles. Dating back to about AD 500, it is the shortest and best-known creed. This creed is rooted in the Old Roman Symbol (or Creed), dating from the second century, with early evidence of it being used in baptismal rites as an interrogatory creed. The creed was broken into three sections (God, Jesus Christ, and Holy Spirit), then presented to the initiate as a question that began with "Do you believe . . ."—to which the response is "I do" or "I believe." Legend associates each sentence with one of the twelve apostles, as shown below, with each statement written by an Apostle after Pentecost, through the inspiration of the Holy Spirit.

I believe in God, the Father almighty,
    creator of heaven and earth.   [St. Peter]
I believe in Jesus Christ, his only Son, our Lord.   [St. Andrew]
    He was conceived by the power of the Holy Spirit
        and born of the Virgin Mary.   [St. James the Great]
    He suffered under Pontius Pilate,
        was crucified, died, and was buried.   [St. John]
    He descended to the dead.
    On the third day he rose again.   [St. Thomas]
    He ascended into heaven,
        and is seated at the right hand of the Father.   [St. James the Less]
    He will come again to judge the living and the dead.   [St. Philip]
I believe in the Holy Spirit,
    the holy catholic Church,   [St. Bartholomew]
    the communion of saints,   [St. Matthew]
    the forgiveness of sins,   [St. Simon]
    the resurrection of the body,   [St. Jude]
    and the life everlasting.   [St. Matthias]
Amen.[71]

THE NICENE CREED

The confession of faith drawn up by the Council of Nicaea in AD 325 and commonly used in the Communion Service and on feast days.

> We believe in one God,
>> the Father, the Almighty,
>> maker of heaven and earth,
>> of all that is, seen and unseen.
> We believe in one Lord, Jesus Christ,
>> the only Son of God,
>> eternally begotten of the Father,
>> God from God, light from light,
>> true God from true God,
>> begotten, not made,
>> of one Being with the Father;
>> through him all things were made.
>> For us and for our salvation
>> he came down from heaven,
>> was incarnate of the Holy Spirit and the Virgin Mary
>> and became truly human.
>> For our sake he was crucified under Pontius Pilate;
>> he suffered death and was buried.
>> On the third day he rose again
>> in accordance with the Scriptures;
>> he ascended into heaven
>> and is seated at the right hand of the Father.
>> He will come again in glory to judge the living and the
>>> dead,
>> and his kingdom will have no end.
> We believe in the Holy Spirit, the Lord, the giver of life,
>> who proceeds from the Father [and the Son],
>> who with the Father and the Son is worshiped
>>> and glorified,

who has spoken through the prophets.
We believe in one holy catholic and apostolic Church.
We acknowledge one baptism for the forgiveness of sins.
We look for the resurrection of the dead,
and the life of the world to come. Amen.[72]

THE CREED OF SAINT ATHANASIUS

(Sometimes called the *Quicunque Vult* or the Athanasian Creed.) The third of the three General Creeds, this originated about AD 400 to combat heretical teachings. It emphasizes the doctrines of the **Trinity** and the **Incarnation**.

Whosoever will be saved, before all things it is necessary
  that he hold the Catholic Faith.
Which Faith except everyone do keep whole and unde-
  filed, without doubt he shall perish everlastingly.
And the Catholic Faith is this: That we worship one God
  in Trinity, and Trinity in Unity, neither confounding
  the Persons, nor dividing the Substance.
For there is one Person of the Father, another of the Son,
  and another of the Holy Ghost.
But the Godhead of the Father, of the Son, and of the
  Holy Ghost, is all one, the Glory equal, the Majesty
  co-eternal.
Such as the Father is, such is the Son, and such is the
  Holy Ghost.
The Father uncreate, the Son uncreate, and the Holy
  Ghost uncreate.
The Father incomprehensible, the Son incomprehensible,
  and the Holy Ghost incomprehensible.
The Father eternal, the Son eternal, and the Holy Ghost
  eternal.

———

183

And yet they are not three eternals, but one eternal.

As also there are not three incomprehensibles, nor three uncreated, but one uncreated, and one incomprehensible.

So likewise the Father is Almighty, the Son Almighty, and the Holy Ghost Almighty.

And yet they are not three Almighties, but one Almighty. So the Father is God, the Son is God, and the Holy Ghost is God.

And yet they are not three Gods, but one God.

So likewise the Father is Lord, the Son Lord, and the Holy Ghost Lord.

And yet not three Lords, but one Lord.

For like as we are compelled by the Christian verity to acknowledge every Person by himself to be both God and Lord,

So are we forbidden by the Catholic Religion, to say, There be three Gods, or three Lords.

The Father is made of none, neither created, nor begotten.

The Son is of the Father alone, not made, nor created, but begotten.

The Holy Ghost is of the Father and of the Son, neither made, nor created, nor begotten, but proceeding.

So there is one Father, not three Fathers; one Son, not three Sons; one Holy Ghost, not three Holy Ghosts.

And in this Trinity none is afore, or after other; none is greater, or less than another;

But the whole three Persons are co-eternal together and co-equal.

So that in all things, as is aforesaid, the Unity in Trinity and the Trinity in Unity is to be worshipped.

He therefore that will be saved must thus think of the Trinity.

Furthermore, it is necessary to everlasting salvation that he also believe rightly the Incarnation of our Lord Jesus Christ.

For the right Faith is, that we believe and confess, that our Lord Jesus Christ, the Son of God, is God and Man;

God, of the Substance of the Father, begotten before the worlds; and Man, of the Substance of his Mother, born in the world;

Perfect God and perfect Man, of a reasonable soul and human flesh subsisting;

Equal to the Father, as touching his Godhead; and inferior to the Father, as touching his Manhood.

Who although he be God and Man, yet he is not two, but one Christ;

One, not by conversion of the Godhead into flesh, but by taking of the Manhood into God;

One altogether; not by confusion of Substance, but by unity of Person.

For as the reasonable soul and flesh is one man, so God and Man is one Christ;

Who suffered for our salvation, descended into hell, rose again the third day from the dead.

He ascended into heaven; he sitteth on the right hand of the Father, God Almighty, from whence he shall come to judge the quick and the dead.

At whose coming all men shall rise again with their bodies and shall give account for their own works.

And they that have done good shall go into life everlasting, and they that have done evil into everlasting fire.

This is the Catholic Faith, which except a man believe faithfully, he cannot be saved.[73]

CONFESSIONS AND
DOCTRINAL STATEMENTS

A **confession** is a formal statement of belief of a church or denomination, such as the following:

Anglican/Episcopal:
> **Thirty-Nine Articles of Religion**. A definition of the faith of the Church of England drawn up in 1571, and included in The Book of Common Prayer.

Lutheran (Martin Luther):
> **Augsburg Confession**. The basic Lutheran confession of faith, largely the work of Philip Melanchthon, an associate of Martin Luther, in 1530.

Presbyterian:
> **Westminster Confession**. A confession of faith of the Presbyterian Church drawn up by the Westminster Assembly in 1643, and still extensively used.

Reformed (John Calvin):
> **Canon of Dort**. A statement of the doctrine of the Reformed Church drawn up by the synod held at Dort in 1618 and 1619.

DOCTRINE

doctrine. The principles or teachings of a religion or denomination as taught and observed by its members. May also be called *dogma*.

atonement. Reconciliation of God and humankind (at-one-ment) through the use of a sin-bearer. In the Old Testament, the sin-bearer was an animal sacrifice. Christ became the sin-bearer through his sacrificial death (Rom. 3:25; Heb. 2:17).

Christian. One who professes belief in Jesus Christ and follows his teachings.

conversion. The turning from sin to God, through belief in Jesus Christ and by the power of the Holy Spirit.

dispensation. Permission given by an authority in the church to do something special. Also, in the eschatological teachings of certain **Protestant** churches, an era of time in which God works and reveals himself in a particular manner for a particular purpose.

evangelical. (From the Greek, *evangel* or "good news.") Those denominations of Christians who emphasize salvation by **faith** alone, without works or ritual (sacrament), and the centrality of the authority of Scripture (rather than tradition).

excommunication. The exclusion of a person from Holy Communion and church membership as a punishment, usually for **heresy**.

faith. Belief and trust in God.

grace. Unmerited favor or kindness, especially the kindness of God to fallen humankind in his provision for human **redemption** through Jesus Christ (Eph. 2:8–9).

heresy. Opinions, doctrines, and beliefs contrary to those taught by the Church.

immortality. The belief that the soul lives on after the death of the body. This is confessed in the **Apostles' Creed** as "the life everlasting," and in the **Nicene Creed** as "the life of the world to come."

incarnation. (Latin, "made flesh.") The Son of God was made flesh and became man, as commemorated on December 25 (John 1:14).

justification. Being placed in a right relationship with God, through the redemptive work of Christ Jesus.

reconciliation. The act of restoring a relationship, specifically the relationship between God and humans, as a result of the redemptive work of Jesus Christ (Rom. 5:10; 2 Cor. 5:19), establishing the foundation for continued fellowship with God. The result is not only the restored relationship between God and humans, but also the restoration of relationships among people. In the Roman Church, **Reconciliation** is the sacrament formerly known as **Penance**. (See also chapter 7, **The Sacraments**.)

redemption. To redeem is to release or free for a price. In God's economy, humankind is redeemed from the consequences of sin (death) through Christ's death, and through his **resurrection**, death was destroyed.

regeneration. Spiritual rebirth, into a life reconciled to God through Christ (John 3:3).

repentance. A change of mind that involves profound change in the direction of life, specifically to turn away from sin and turn to God for grace (Acts 20:21).

Resurrection. The event of Christ's return to life after his death by crucifixion as witnessed by his followers. See also **resurrection of the dead**.

revival. Spiritual rebirth or reawakening usually associated with the work of the Holy Spirit (2 Kings 18:1–7; Acts 19:17–20).

GOD

How to define the indefinable? According to the Westminster Larger Catechism, "God is a Spirit, in and of himself infinite in being, glory, blessedness, and perfection; all-sufficient, eternal, unchangeable, incomprehensible, everywhere present, almighty, knowing all things, most wise, most holy, most just, most merciful and gracious, long-suffering, and abundant in goodness and truth." Or perhaps, "God is the supreme and supremely personal Source and Creator of the universe, revealed in creation and in the events of salvation history (covenant, prophecy, the Incarnation of Jesus Christ, and the ongoing presence of the Holy Spirit), an object of religious devotion and subject matter of theology."

SOME NAMES OF GOD

El is the generic Semitic name for "God" or "deity" and one of the oldest names for God used in the ancient world. The root meaning is "power and authority" (Gen. 1:1; Ps. 19:1).

Eloah is a singular form of *Elohim*, used primarily in Job (42 times). *Elohim* is the plural form of *El* and *Eloah,* used overwhelmingly (more than 2,300 times) in the Old Testament to refer to the God of Israel, meaning "the true God." *Theos* is the Greek counterpart of *Elohim* (cf. Matt. 22:32 and Exod. 3:6) and usually refers to the true God.

El Elyon "Most High" (Gen. 14:18–20)

El Elohe-Yisra'el "God, the God of Israel" (Gen. 33:20)

El Shaddai "God the Mountain" (Gen. 49:25)

El Olam "God the Everlasting One" or "God of Eternity" (Gen. 21:33)

Adonai, Adon or *Adonay* is a title of respect that emphasizes God's sovereignty, that is "Lord." The word *Adonai* belongs preeminently to *Yahweh*, for he alone is the "Lord of the earth" (Josh. 3:11, 13). It was after the Exile (538 BC) that the name

189

Yahweh (which was considered too holy to be said aloud) began to be pronounced as *Adonai* during the reading of the Scriptures. *Kurios* is the Greek counterpart of both *Adonai* (cf. Matt. 22:44 and Ps. 110:1) and *Yahweh* (cf. Matt. 4:10 and Deut. 6:13), used in both the New Testament and the Septuagint.

Yahweh is the personal covenant name of Israel's God, the most common name for God used 6,829 times in the Old Testament. **Yah** is the shortened form. Most Bible translations show *Yahweh* as LORD or LORD, to distinguish it from other names of God. The name sounds like and may be derived from the Hebrew for the word "I AM" (Exod. 3:14–15), meaning "He who is" or "He who is truly present" or "I will be to you all that I am." The actual meaning (and the correct pronunciation) of the name Yahweh itself remains a mystery.

The significance of this name and what makes it more holy and revered than other names is that this is God's intensely personal name, the one he revealed as his own. He is not merely one god among many: *Yahweh* is the "Creator and Ruler of heaven and earth, who is worthy of and demands the exclusive homage of his people." His name is so sacred that out of fear and respect it is not pronounced. Jesus echoed the name of God, *Yahweh*, "I AM" in his **seven "I am's."** And when Jesus identified himself with *Yahweh* in John 8:58: "I tell you the truth, before Abraham was born, I am!" his listeners understood immediately and without question his reference to the self-revelation of God to Moses (Exod. 3:14).

Some specific uses of the name Yahweh are as follows:

Yahweh Nissi "Yahweh is my banner or standard" (Exod. 17:8–15)
Yahweh Shalom "Yahweh is peace" (Judg. 6:23–24)
Yahweh Tsabbaoth "LORD of Hosts" or "LORD Almighty" (1 Sam. 17:45)
Yahweh Tsidkenu "Yahweh our Righteousness" (Jer. 23:5–6)
Yahweh Yireh (*Jireh*) "Yahweh will provide" (Gen. 22:14; cf. v. 8)

190

SYMBOLS OF GOD

All-seeing Eye. A symbol of the omniscience of God (Ps. 33:18). The eye is shown within a rayed triangle.

circle. This is an ancient symbol representing eternity and completeness because it has no beginning and no ending.

Creator's star. A six-pointed star, made from two equilateral triangles, symbolizing the Triune God. The six points are reminiscent of the six attributes of God: Power, Majesty, Wisdom, Love, Mercy, and Justice, and also of the six days of Creation.

hand of God (*Manus Dei*). A symbol of God the Father, the only symbol for God used during the first eight centuries of the church. The hand symbolizes God as creator and sustainer of all of creation, and comes from the many references to the "hand of God" in the Bible (e.g., Deut. 3:23–24; Ezra 8:21–23; 1 Pet. 5:6). The Hand may be shown in any of the following postures:
- reaching down from the clouds.
- descending from the clouds, and holding five tiny human beings, representative of being held in God's hand (Ps. 139:10).
- in the Latin form, reaching down from heaven in blessing, the two first fingers and thumb extended, and the other two bent to the palm. This image is superimposed over a three-rayed **nimbus** enclosed in a circle, a symbol of Deity.
- in the Greek form, with the hand pointing to heaven, the forefinger extended, the middle finger and little finger closed in a half-circle, and the thumb crossing the ring finger. Reading right to left, this form spells ICXC, or *Jesus Christ* in Greek.

JESUS CHRIST, THE SON OF GOD

The person known as Jesus of Nazareth, recognized by Christians as the Christ, who was crucified, died, buried, and rose from the dead, and is called the Son of God incarnate. The name "Jesus" is the anglicized version of the Greek *Iesous,* for the Hebrew *Yeshua, Jehoshua,* or *Joshua,* or "Yahweh is salvation."

MONOGRAMS OF JESUS

Alpha and Omega. Alpha is the first letter of the Greek alphabet, and Omega is the last, and together they symbolize the eternal nature of Christ (Rev. 1:8). They may appear as distinct letters or joined in a monogram, but are never seen apart from each other.

Chi Rho. A Christogram from the first two letters of *XPICTOC* (pronounced "Christos"). These Greek letters, XP, are familiar symbols on **paraments**. Also seen as a Chi Rho in joined rings, a Chi Rho with the Alpha and Omega, or as a circle containing the Chi Rho with the Alpha and Omega.

IHC or **IHS**. The first three letters of "Jesus" in Greek. A monogram of his name, the IHC being the older form. It does not mean "In His Sign."

IC XC. Monograms created from the first and last letters of the Greek words "Jesus" and "Christ." Often appears with a cross and the word **NIKA**, meaning Jesus Christ the Conqueror.

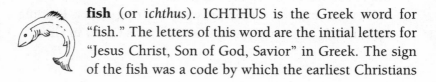

fish (or *ichthus*). ICHTHUS is the Greek word for "fish." The letters of this word are the initial letters for "Jesus Christ, Son of God, Savior" in Greek. The sign of the fish was a code by which the earliest Christians

---

192

identified themselves to one another in the days of persecution. It also recalls the sacrament of **Holy Baptism** (a fish must live in water) and is thus a symbol of Christian regeneration. The circle of three fish symbolizes baptism in the name of the **Trinity**.

SOME NAMES OF OUR LORD JESUS CHRIST

King of Kings or the **Kingly Christ.** The painted or carved figure of Christ on the cross wearing eucharistic vestments and a crown (Rev. 17:14; 19:16; see also Deut. 10:17; Ps. 136:2–3; Dan. 2:47; 1 Tim. 6:15).

Good Shepherd. Jesus Christ's own description of himself and his work, as recorded in John 10:11. The image of a shepherd carrying a lamb on his shoulders was common in the Early Church, particularly in the catacombs and other burial sites, and was adapted from the ancient Greek and Roman burial symbol of Orpheus, who was pictured holding a lyre or with a sheep on his shoulders.

Lamb of God. From John the Baptist's proclamation about Jesus (John 1:29, 36).

Messiah. (Hebrew, "The Anointed One.") The long-awaited king and deliverer of Israel, prophesied in the Hebrew Scriptures. "Messiah" is translated as "Christ" in Greek, and both terms were used by followers of Jesus and acknowledged by Jesus himself (Matt. 16:15–20; Mark 14:61–63; John 1:41).

the seven "I am's." Statements made by Jesus Christ that reveal his character and his work. All come from the Gospel of John.
- I am the bread of life (6:35);
- I am the light of the world (8:12), often symbolized by a candle;
- I am the door (10:9);

- I am the good shepherd (10:11, 14), often symbolized by a shepherd's staff or a shepherd holding a lamb;

  - I am the resurrection and the life (11:25);
  - I am the way, the truth, and the life (14:6);
  - I am the true vine (15:1, 5), often symbolized by a vine and branches. The vine represents Christ and the branches, his followers. The symbol is a popular one in ecclesiastical embroidery and carving.

SYMBOLS OF OUR LORD JESUS CHRIST

Agnus Dei. (Latin, "Lamb of God.") A lamb as an emblem of Christ. The Suffering Lamb is shown with a cross, the Triumphal Lamb with a waving banner, and the Enthroned Lamb seated on the Book of Seven Seals (Rev. 5:6–14). From the words of John the Baptist in John 1:29, 36.

anchor. A symbol of Christian hope, with Christ as the "anchor for the soul" (Heb. 6:19). One of our earliest Christian symbols, found in the catacombs, and one of the symbols Christians used to communicate with each other. Sometimes used with a cross and a heart to represent faith, hope, and love. Also appears in depictions of St. Clement as a symbol of his martydom.

brazen serpent or bronze snake. The brazen serpent on a cross is a symbol of the crucifixion (John 3:14–15), recalling God's

SYMBOLS OF OUR LORD JESUS CHRIST

"KING OF KINGS"   "LIGHT OF THE WORLD"   *"AGNUS DEI"* "LAMB OF GOD"   "ANCHOR OF THE SOUL"   "THE SUFFERING SAVIOUR"

"CROWN OF LIFE"   "CROWN OF THORNS"

instructions to Moses for healing the Israelites from venomous snake bites (Num. 21:8–9).

crown. The symbol of sovereignty, it represents Christ as Lord, the King of kings. The **crown of thorns** is a passion symbol of Jesus, representing the suffering Savior. The symbol of the crown also represents the reward of the faithful Christian life (1 Pet. 5:4).

halo. See **nimbus**.

lamb. As in the Old Testament a lamb was sacrificed, so in the New Testament, Christ was the sacrificial victim, the lamb. See *Agnus Dei*.

lion (with a three-rayed nimbus). Symbol of Christ, "the Lion of the tribe of Judah" (Rev. 5:5).

nimbus. (Latin, "cloud.") Deity is indicated with a nimbus from which three rays are emanating or a circular nimbus containing three rays. Images pictured with a three-rayed nimbus are symbolic of Jesus. Jesus himself may be shown with a ring-shaped halo, or may be surrounded completely by an aureole.

scepter. The sign of ruling authority. See also **chapter 3, The Cross.**

HOLY SPIRIT

(Or, *Holy Ghost*.) The third Person of the **Holy Trinity**, distinct from the Father and the Son (Jesus), but of the same substance, co-equal and co-eternal. The Holy Spirit is at work in the world today, sent by Jesus to empower and provide guidance to the Church (John 14:16–26). The Holy Spirit is called the *Paraclete*, which is translated consoler, counselor, advocate, and comforter, all descriptive of the Holy Spirit's work in the lives of believers, and the source of the name the *Holy Comforter*.

According to Isaiah 11:2, the gifts of the Holy Spirit are wisdom, understanding, counsel, power, knowledge, and fear of the Lord. According to Paul, the gifts of the Holy Spirit to the Body of Christ are wisdom, knowledge, faith, healing, miracles, prophecy, discernment, apostleship, teaching, administration, tongues, and interpretation of tongues, and most important, love (1 Cor. 12, 13, 14). The fruits of the Holy Spirit (evidence of his work in a Christian's life) are love, joy, peace, patience, kindness, goodness, faithfulness, gentleness, and self-control (Gal. 5:22–23).

SYMBOLS OF THE HOLY SPIRIT

dove. The descending dove represents peace and purity and is a symbol of the Holy Spirit. In many instances, a dove is pictured with a three-rayed nimbus, identifying it as the Holy Spirit, a member of the **Holy Trinity**. The dove may be found on the cover of a font and in pictures of our Lord's baptism, signifying the Spirit's descent in the form of a dove as Jesus emerged from the water (Matt. 3:16; Mark 1:10; Luke 3:22; and John 1:32).

flames or **fire.** When the Holy Spirit descended upon the disciples at **Pentecost**, he came in the form of tongues of fire which came to rest upon their heads, empowering them to spread the gospel (Acts 2:1–4). The red that is worn on Pentecost Sunday symbolizes fire.

SS. Abbreviation for *Spiritus Sanctus*, Latin for "Holy Spirit." Sometimes abbreviated as *Spus Scus*.

wild goose. From the Celtic tradition. This is not the serene and calm Holy Spirit of the dove; it is rather the Holy Spirit with the raucous, demanding, and unsettling nature of the wild goose.

HOLY TRINITY

The Triune God, consisting of God the Father, God the Son, and God the Holy Spirit.

SYMBOLS OF THE HOLY TRINITY

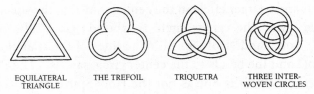

EQUILATERAL TRIANGLE   THE TREFOIL   TRIQUETRA   THREE INTER-WOVEN CIRCLES

circle enclosing a triangle. The circle represents eternity and completeness, and the triangle enclosed in a circle symbolizes the Holy Trinity.

fleur-de-lis. Three parts, one flower.

interwoven circles (**interlaced**). Three interwoven circles represent the unity of the Triune God, and a cross enclosed in a circle means eternal life.

Sanctus, Sanctus, Sanctus, or the initials **SSS**. (Latin, "Holy, Holy, Holy.") Sometimes these words appear in art, symbolizing the Holy Trinity.

three fishes. Linked together in the shape of a triangle.

trefoil. Saint Patrick used a shamrock to illustrate the nature of the Holy Trinity, and the image of three equal lobes found its way into church symbolism, especially in architecture and embroidery. Whether used alone or combined with a circle or **triangle**, it always symbolizes the Trinity.

triangle. Only an equilateral triangle is used in ecclesiastical art because it signifies that the Holy Trinity—Father, Son, and Holy Spirit—are equal, yet one. Usually a line drawing, the triangle also may be made of three fish, one forming each side.

The triangle forms the foundation of the *Shield of the Holy Trinity*, which shows an inverted triangle with a small circle at each point and a larger circle in the center, joined to the small ones by double lines. The center circle is labeled "God," the others "Father," "Son," and "Holy Spirit." The lines of the triangle each say "is not" and the bands to the center circle say "is." The Father is not the Son, and the Son is not the Holy Spirit, and the Holy Spirit is not the Father, but each is God.

triquetra. Formed by three intersecting and interwoven arcs, this ancient symbol is seen in the some of the earliest paintings of Jesus and the Evangelists and on stone crosses found in Great Britain dating from its early days of Christianity. From this image, the nature of the Trinity is shown: the equality of the Three Persons, from the equal length of the arcs; the eternity of God, seen in its continuous form; and the indivisibility of God, in its interwoven arcs. In addition a triangle is formed at the center and a **vesica** by each pair of arcs.

vesica. A pointed "fish" shape made by the intersection of segments of two circles. This is the shape of the aureole that surrounds the Madonna and Child. This form is often used on the back of the **chasuble**.

SIN, TEMPTATION & DEATH:
THE WORLD, THE FLESH, & THE DEVIL

brambles, briars, thistles, thorns. Among the results of Adam and Eve's sin was that the ground was cursed to bring forth thorns and thistles (Gen. 3:17–19). In Scripture, these weeds speak of the results of sin and idolatry. They often symbolize sin itself, and worldly interests and cares.

bellows. Symbolizes temptation. Sometimes shown with the devil sending out blasts of temptation.

earth (orb), encircled by a serpent. The world bound in sin.

fiery arrows (or **darts**). From Eph. 6:16. Represents temptation of the devil; also persecution.

handcuffs or **fetters.** The bondage of sin; the power of Satan; the power of hell. Broken fetters represent sin overcome.

leaven (yeast). This image was used by Jesus to describe the pervasive (and evil) influence of the religious leaders (Matt. 16:6–12). Also represents the kingdom of heaven, especially the influence of Christian Church (Matt. 13:33).

lion. The devil is sometimes represented as a roaring lion (1 Pet. 5:8).

scorpion. Evil, treachery, and by extension, sin and the work of the devil. Sometimes associated with Judas, and shown on the flags of the Roman soldiers who crucified Jesus Christ.

serpent, snake, viper. Satan, the Fall (Gen. 3:1–7), sin.

Seven Deadly Sins. Pride, anger, covetousness, lust, envy, sloth, and gluttony.

sin. Sin is that which separates us from God, our revolt against the holiness of God and his sovereign will. It involves the heart, mind, will, and affections, everything we are, and is evident in our thoughts and actions. Sin is at once the evidence of our humanity (through sinful actions) and a condition of our humanity (through Original Sin). *Original Sin* refers to the sin that humankind inherited as a result of the disobedience of Adam and Eve, which brought on the total corruption of the whole human nature and of creation (Genesis 3; Rom. 5:12–21).

skull. Death. Associated specifically with Adam and the Fall. When shown under the crucified Savior, it represents Adam's skull, and so his sin, defeated by Jesus Christ.

LAST THINGS

eschatology. (Greek, "words about last things.") Doctrines dealing with last things, such as death, resurrection, the second coming of Jesus Christ, divine judgment, and the end of this age and the future. The Old Testament speaks of a future resurrection and judgment (Job 19:25–27; Isa. 25:6–9; Dan. 12:1–3); the New Testament expands on this teaching by including resurrection (Rom. 8:11; 1 Corinthians 15), the second coming of Christ (Matt. 16:27; Luke 17:30; 1 Thess. 4:13–18; 1 Pet. 1:7; 1 John 2:28), and the final judgment when the wicked are cast into hell (Rev. 20:11–15) and the righteous enter heaven (Matt. 25:31–46).

antichrist. An enemy of Christ or someone who usurps his name and rights through brute force, lawlessness, and deceit. Though the word is found only in four verses in the New Testament (1 John 2:18, 22; 4:3; 2 John 7), the concept of a person or power who sets himself against Messiah/Christ and pretends to be God is found throughout Scripture. Called the *"man of lawlessness"* by Paul (2 Thess. 2:1–12), and associated with the beast of Daniel 7–8 and Revelation (Rev. 13:11–18; 17:8).

Apocalypse. From the Greek word for "revelation." A name used for the book of Revelation, which describes the return of Jesus Christ and the Final Judgment. Literature that describes similar events is called *apocalyptic literature* (the book of Daniel, for example). This word is also used in 2 Thess. 1:6–8 in Paul's description of God's final judgment: ". . . when the Lord Jesus is revealed from heaven in blazing fire with his powerful angels."

Armageddon. The name given to the final battle between the forces of good and the forces of evil, used only once in Scripture (Rev. 16:16). The word probably finds its roots in the name *Har Mageddon*, "the mountain of Megiddo." The Valley of Jezreel and the Plain of Esdraelon, located at the foot of Mt. Megiddo, were the sites of many decisive battles in the history of Israel (Judg. 5:19–20; 6:33; 1 Samuel 31 and 2 Sam. 4:4; 2 Kings 9:27; 2 Kings 23:29–30).

balances or **scales.** Refers to the weighing of souls or the Day of Judgment. May be shown with human figures on one pan or with the devil pulling down one pan. St. Michael the Archangel is often portrayed carrying the scales of justice.

Day of Judgment (*Judgment Day, Day of Reckoning, Last Judgment*). The day when nations and individuals will be judged by Jesus Christ, in which he will examine the deeds and motives of all persons, believer and unbeliever (Matt. 11:20–22; 12:36; 25:35–40; 2 Cor. 5:10). The term also refers to the human response to God as he is revealed to each (Matt. 16:27; Rom. 1:18–21; Rev. 20:12).

Day of the Lord. Described in both the Old and New Testaments as the day when God will deliver Israel and the Church, and triumph over his foes. It begins with the Second Coming of Jesus Christ, accompanied by cataclysmic social and physical events (Matthew 24; Luke 21:7–33). It also includes the judgment (Rev. 4:1–19:6), and culminates finally in the creation of the new heaven and the new earth (Isa. 65:17; 66:22; Rev. 21:1). The Day of the Lord is regarded as an imminent event, and the righteous are encouraged to prepare and stay ready (Zeph. 1:14–15; 2 Thess. 2:2).

Doom. A painting, carving, or other representation of the Last Judgment, which includes Jesus Christ weighing souls and sending them either to heaven or to hell.

doomsday or **Doom's Day.** The Day of Judgment. The root of the word "doom" is found in an Old English word for law, judgment, or condemnation.

fire. God's judgment or vengeance is said to be delivered by fire (Jer. 23:29; Mal. 3:2; Luke 12:49; Rev. 20:9), especially the destruction of the wicked (Matt. 13:42, 50; 25:41; Mark 9:48; Rev. 9:2; 21:8). Also speaks of everlasting or eternal punishment, as hell or Hades or fire and brimstone (Matt. 18:8; 25:41; Mark 9:48). Fire may also symbolize spiritual power (Jer. 20:9; Luke 3:16) and cleansing (Isa. 6:6–7). Fire also represents the **Holy Spirit**.

earthquake. Both a judgment (Ps. 60:2; Isa. 13:13; 24:18–20; 29:6; Nah. 1:5; Rev. 6:12–14; 16:18, 20) and a prophetic sign of pending judgment (Zech. 14:4; Matt. 24:7; Rev. 11:19).

famine. Both judgment (Jer. 14:12, 15; Ezek. 5:16) and a prophetic sign of pending judgment (Matt. 24:4–8).

fishing net. Signifies the final judgment when all the fish will be gathered in a net to be sorted, and the bad fish thrown away (Matt. 13:47–50).

Four Last Things. Death, judgment, heaven, hell.

Four Horsemen of the Apocalypse. From Revelation 6:1–8. The imagery of the four horsemen comes from Zechariah 1:8–17; 6:1–8.
- white horse symbolizes conquest; its rider carries a bow and is given a crown;
- red horse symbolizes bloodshed and war (as in Zech. 1:8; 6:2); its rider carries a sword;
- black horse symbolizes famine (as in Zech. 6:2, 6); its rider carries a pair of scales;
- pale horse, recalling the ashen appearance of the dead, symbolizes death and judgment.

gate. In art may speak of entering or exiting, either Paradise or Hell.

heaven. The dwelling place of God (Isa. 66:1) and of the good angels (Matt. 24:36), and where his redeemed will someday live in his presence. May also be called *Paradise*.

hell. Described in the Bible as both a place and a state of eternal punishment after death, a situation of suffering in eternal separation from God, considered the reward of the wicked. Sometimes referred to as *Hades* (the Greek word for the abode of the dead in Greek mythology) or *Sheol* (the Hebrew word for the same).

kingdom of God (or kingdom of heaven). God's sovereign rule in which evil is defeated and sinners are redeemed. It is ruled by Christ, who will destroy all his enemies (including death) and then deliver the kingdom to the Father (1 Cor. 15:24–26). The kingdom of God is both now and in the future, and includes all who submit voluntarily to the rule of God in their lives, beginning with the new birth (John 3:3–5). "Kingdom of God" is used throughout the New Testament, but "kingdom of heaven" is used only in Matthew.

lightning. A symbol of God's power and an instrument of God's vengeance or the destruction of his enemies (Ps. 18:14; 144:6; Zech. 9:14–15).

mark of the beast. An image that could find its origin in the ancient tradition of branding slaves and captured enemy soldiers or in the sealing and stamping of official documents. Refers to the allegiance that will be demanded by the antichrist in his final days (Rev. 13:11–17; 14:9, 11; 15:2; 16:2; 19:20; 20:4). Also echoes the seal of baptism, the sign of the cross on the forehead.

millennium. Latin for "a thousand years," described in Rev. 20:1–15. During this period, Christ will rule and Satan will be bound. It is a time of peace, when Jesus shall have triumphed over all forms of evil (1 Cor. 15:24–28; 2 Thess. 2:8; Rev. 14:6–18; 19:11–16) and when creation shall be liberated from the corruption of evil (Rom. 8:19–21). The Son of Man shall sit on the throne of his glory (Matt. 19:28; Luke 22:28–30), and the righteous shall rule with him (Dan. 7:22; Matt. 19:28; Luke 22:28–30; 1 Cor. 6:2). Christ will rule from his throne in Zion or Jerusalem (Isa. 65:17–25; Zech. 9:9–10), fulfilling the promise of the kingdom of God on earth (Matt. 26:29; Heb. 8:11).

Paradise. Heaven; or the Garden of Eden.

plague. Calamities sent by God as judgment. Used on the Egyptians (Exodus 7–12), and as part of God's future judgment (Revelation 16).

purgatory. (Roman Church only.) A time of suffering after death during which souls make amends for their sins before entering heaven.

resurrection of the dead. Affirmed in the Creeds, the return to life of all human life before God's final judgment (Isa. 26:19; Dan. 12:2; John 5:28–29; Acts 24:15; 1 Cor. 15:20–21; Rev. 20:13). See also **Resurrection** (of Jesus Christ).

666. The number of the **beast** or **Antichrist** (Rev. 13:18).

scythe or sickle. A farming instrument used to mow or reap. Symbolic of destruction and death, as in the harvest of souls (Rev. 14:14–20).

Second Coming. The personal, visible, and glorious return of Jesus Christ (Matt. 24:30; Acts 1:11; 3:19–21; Phil. 3:20).

sheep and goats. The redeemed and the lost, separated on the Day of Judgment (Matt. 25:32–33).

signs. Both the Old and New Testament state that signs of God's judgment and Christ's return will be shown in the sun, moon, and stars (Joel 2:30–31; Isa. 13:10; Matt. 24:29, 35; Mark 13:24–25; Luke 21:25; Acts 2:19–20; Rev. 8:10–12).

Tribulation. A time of suffering (including war, famine, and plagues) sent from God upon the earth for its wickedness. A precursor of Christ's return (Dan. 12:1; Matt. 24:21; Rev. 7:14).

trumpet, held by an angel. Heralds God's judgment (Rev. 8:7–11:19) and the resurrection of the dead (1 Thess. 4:16–17).

volcano. In art, represents divine judgment.

war, famine, and plagues. Both judgment for disobedience (Lev. 26:14–26) and prophetic signs of pending judgment (Matt. 24:4–8).

wheat and tares (or *weeds*). Represents the Day of Judgment, when believers and unbelievers are separated for their reward (Matt. 13:24–30, 36–43).

wine press. Image of the wrath of God, especially, the Day of the Lord (Isa. 63:3; Lam. 1:15; Joel 3:13; Rev. 14:17–20; 19:15–16).

ELEVEN

The Body of Christ

THE CHURCH UNIVERSAL

The primary and exclusive aim of the liturgy is not the expression of the individual's reverence and worship for God. It is not even concerned with the awakening, formation and sanctification of the individual soul as such. Nor does the onus of liturgical action and prayer rest with the individual. It does not even rest with the collective groups, composed of numerous individuals, who periodically achieve a limited and intermittent unity in their capacity as the congregation of a church. The liturgical entity consists rather of the united body of the faithful as such—the church—a body which infinitely outnumbers the mere congregation. (Romano Guardini)[74]

The word *church* is from the Greek *kuriakos*, "belonging to the Lord," but is used also to translate another Greek word, *ekklesia*, "assembly" (the root of the word *ecclesiastical*). It is used in the New Testament to denote both a local Christian community (Gal. 1:2; 1 Thess. 1:1) and the whole Christian community (1 Cor. 12:28). Other designations in the New Testament for the Church are the *Body of Christ* or *Christ's body* (Rom. 12:5; 1 Cor. 12:27; Eph. 1:22–23; 4:12; Col. 1:24) and the *Bride* or *Bride of Christ* (Eph. 5:25–26; Rev. 21:9). In general, when the word "Church" is capitalized, it refers to the entire body of Christ, and when it is in lower case, it refers to a local **congregation**.

Church Militant. The Church on earth, fighting evil.

Church Triumphant. Those members of the Church who have triumphed and now live in God's glory.

catholic. "Universal" or embracing all Christians, as it is meant in the words of the creed "the holy catholic church." When used in reference to the universal Church, the word may or may not be capitalized, but when used as an abbreviated term for the Roman Catholic Church, it is always capitalized.

communicant. A baptized and confirmed member in good standing who receives the **Holy Communion**.

communion of saints. All the faithful of the Church in communion with each other and with Christ.

THE HISTORICAL CHURCH

apostle. (Greek, "messenger.") The term specifically denoting the Twelve whom Jesus trained and sent forth as apostles (Mark 3:14; Luke 6:13). Paul later became known as an apostle, although he was not one of the Twelve. The word *apostle* was also used more generally in the New Testament (Rom. 16:7; Gal. 1:19) and is considered to be a spiritual gift available in the church today (1 Cor. 12:28).

apostolic succession. The uninterrupted transmission of authority given by Christ in his pastoral charge to the **Apostles** (John 20:21–23). This authority has been transmitted from the Apostles to the present-day clergy by the laying on of hands at **ordination**.

convention. A meeting of clerical and lay delegates from a large area to conduct the affairs of the church.

council. A convention of church leaders convened to determine matters of doctrine, etc., such as the Council of Nicaea in AD 325, which drafted the **Nicene Creed**. The Council of Jerusalem (Acts 15) was the first church council. The Second Vatican Council (Vatican II) is the most recent council of the Roman Catholic Church.

disciple. A follower or student of a teacher, specifically a follower of Jesus, one who accompanied him during his ministry on earth. Followers of Jesus in the early Church were also called disciples (Acts 6:1–2, 7; 9:36). Today, new Christians are often encouraged to attend discipleship classes, as students of the teachings of Jesus Christ. See **apostle**.

evangelist. (Greek, "proclaimer of good news.") Any person who spreads the gospel. One of the specified gifts of the Holy Spirit (Eph. 4:11). Also, "**Evangelist**" specifically refers to the writers of the "good news" of the Gospels: Matthew, Mark, Luke, and John.

missionary. An ordained or lay person who is sent by a church to spread the gospel at home or abroad. This work primarily involves evangelizing and teaching new believers, but may also include serving local communities by providing medical care and education. Jesus sent out his disciples to preach and heal (Matt. 10:1–15) and commissioned them to go to all nations (Matt. 28:19–20). The Acts of the Apostles records the missionary journeys of Paul and other early believers.

witness. To speak publicly about God's word and work.

CHURCH ORGANIZATION

congregational. The form of church government in which each individual **congregation** or local church is fully self-governing. In this form of church government, authority rests in the local congregation, particularly the power to ordain.

ecumenical. Pertaining to the entire body of churches. Particularly, a movement to promote Christian unity or cooperation all over the world.

episcopal. The form of church organization in which authority rests with the clergy, who are organized into hierarchies of **bishops**. The power to ordain rests with the bishop alone.

evangelical. (Greek, "gospel.") Those denominations of Christians who emphasize salvation by faith rather than through good works or sacraments.

presbyterian. The form of church organization that mixes hierarchical and democratic elements, with power balanced between **clergy** and **laity**. Rather than a hierarchy of **bishops**, there is a hierarchy of churches and governing bodies. Local churches are governed by a ruling body called a *session* or *consistory*, which is composed of the **pastor** and elected **elders**. **Congregations** in turn belong to a *presbytery*, which governs all the congregations in a particular geographic area. In this form of church government, authority is balanced between local congregations and the governing bodies. The power to ordain lies with the presbytery.

Protestant. A term for those churches that arose out of the Reformation. Although beginning as an effort to reform the Church, the Reformation evolved into a widespread "protest" to the Roman Catholic Church of the day. Protestant doctrine emphasizes justification by faith alone, the primary authority of the Bible, and the priesthood of all believers.

seminary. A school for the training of candidates for the **ministry**. A college degree is generally a prerequisite for admission to this three- or four-year course of study.

HIERARCHY

archbishop. The title of a **bishop** who superintends all church matters in a given region.

bishop. (Greek, "overseer.") The chief pastor (overseer)  of a **diocese**. He or she is elected and consecrated as a successor to the Apostles. (See **apostolic succession**.) The bishop is enthroned in a **cathedral**. Among a bishop's duties are **ordination** and **confirmation**. A bishop's insignia include a **throne, miter, ring,** and **crozier**.

chapter. The body of clergy that serves a **cathedral**.

dean. The cleric who serves as the head of the **chapter** at a **cathedral** church. Also a Roman Catholic priest who supervises one district of a diocese.

diocese. The defined territory over which a bishop has jurisdiction. May also be called a *see*. Several dioceses are called a *province*.

prelate. An ecclesiastic of superior rank, such as a **bishop** or **abbot**.

LOCAL CHURCHES

congregation. An assembly of people who meet for worship, fellowship, and instruction. In most cases, these are legally constituted associations of believers, which hold property and assemble for public worship.

parish. A church, or churches, which operates under a charter from the state, maintains its own building, and supports a **pastor** who ministers to its members. Sometimes called a *charge* or a *cure*.

THE CLERGY

The **clergy** are those ordained to the service of God, especially to act as ministers of the gospel and to perform pastoral and sacramental functions in the church.

Secular clergy are clergy whose work brings them into contact with the world, such as parish priests. **Regular clergy** are those who have withdrawn from the world, as in a monastic order. There are various names for the clergy, among which are the following: churchman, cleric, divine, ecclesiast, ecclesiastic, **minister**, parson, **preacher**, reverend, **chaplain**, **curate**, **pastor**, **vicar**, father, **priest**, shepherd.

SECULAR CLERGY

celebrant. The cleric who presides at the Eucharistic celebration.

chaplain. A cleric who ministers to the religious needs of a group other than an organized congregation, such as a military unit, school, institution, etc. The building in which the chaplain conducts services is usually a chapel.

curate. (From Latin, *cure*, "care.") A cleric who serves in a parish as a pastor or an assistant to the pastor or rector.

---

deacon. (Greek, "servant.") In the Eastern Orthodox Church, the Roman Catholic Church, and the Anglican church, a deacon is one ordained to minister to and be the voice of the poor and needy, as in the Early Church (Acts 6:1–7). A deacon's role is to serve and assist the priest, to proclaim the Gospel, to issue invitations (such as to exchange the sign of the peace), and to bear the chalice at the Eucharist. In most Protestant churches, the deacon is a layperson elected to serve in a local church in matters of worship, pastoral care, and administrative work, who usually serves on a board of deacons.

minister. A person ordained to serve a church or ministry. Used especially in Protestant churches.

ministry. The office of those ordained to be the agents of God on earth.

officiant. An ordained minister who conducts the service and administers the sacraments of the church.

pastor. (Latin, "shepherd.") One who serves as the shepherd or spiritual overseer of a local church or **parish**.

preacher. Specifically, the cleric who preaches the sermon.

precentor. (Latin, *praecentor*, "first singer.") A person, usually a member of the clergy, in charge of preparing worship services.

presbyter. (Greek, "elder.") An overseer in the early Christian church; or a priest in churches that have episcopal hierarchies.

priest. Any ordained cleric, but especially one of the Anglican, Eastern Orthodox, or Roman Catholic Church.

rector. The cleric in charge of a **parish**. Term used in the Anglican church.

sacristan. The person in charge of the **sacristy** and ceremonial equipment.

sexton. The person who cares for the church property and attends to other minor duties, such as ringing the **bells** for services.

sister. A woman who has been consecrated to the work of the Lord. In Protestant churches she may be a deaconess with the title "Sister" before her first name. In the Roman Catholic, Anglican, and Lutheran churches, she may be a member of a religious order.

verger. (From Latin, *virga*, "rod.") A position associated largely with cathedrals, an attendant who walks before the bishop carrying a rod (*virge*). A verger's responsibilities originated as a protector of the procession and have developed to include maintaining order during services and seeing to the details of cathedral services, including serving as an **usher** (for dignitaries) and as a **sacristan**.

vicar. An assistant minister or a cleric who serves in the **rector's** stead. May also be the representative of a **prelate**.

REGULAR CLERGY

abbot, abbess. An *abbey* is an autonomous, self-sufficient monastery of at least twelve persons governed by an abbot or an abbess. Addressed as *Father* or *Mother* by members of the community.

brother. A layman consecrated to the religious life, generally through a monastic community, following a rule of poverty, chastity, and obedience.

monk. Commonly used of a man who is a vowed member of a religious community following the monastic rule of life.

novice. A person in the probationary period (called *novitiate*), preparing for first vows in a religious order.

nun. A member of a religious order who lives in a **cloister** and follows vows of poverty, chastity, and obedience through a life of silence, contemplation, and prayer. Some today do not live in a cloister. Often called and addressed as "Sister."

postulant. A candidate for the novitiate in a religious order, participating in a formal program of preparation called *postulancy*.

prior, prioress. A *priory* is the name given to a type of monastic residence governed by a prior or prioress. Also, the superior who ranks next to an abbot or abbess may be called a prior or prioress. Addressed as *Father* or *Mother* by members of the community.

LITURGICAL SERVERS

acolyte. (Greek, "one who follows.") A person, often a youth, who wears a **cassock** and **cotta** or other vestments and assists in the service. Among the duties of acolytes are lighting and extinguishing the candles, finding the pages of the proper Scripture readings, distributing and receiving the **offering plates**, and assisting the celebrant ministering at the **altar** and in the **sanctuary**. (Before girls were permitted to serve, the acolyte was more often called an *altar boy*.)

choir. The organized company of singers who help with the music of the service. A member of the choir is called a *chorister*. (Also refers to the place in the church where the singers or clergy sit.)

crucifer or **cross-bearer.** The person who carries the **processional cross** in the procession.

lay eucharistic minister. A layperson who serves during Holy Communion.

lay reader. An layperson who reads the lessons and assists the priest during the services.

subdeacon. A cleric who ranks below a deacon, whose liturgical responsibilities include serving as a reader and assisting the priest. In the Eastern Orthodox Church, a subdeacon is a member of a minor order. In the Roman Church, the subdeacon was formerly a member of an order, but the position has been discontinued and the functions of reader and acolyte are now performed by lay readers.

thurifer. The person who carries the **censer** in the procession.

LAITY

The **laity** (Greek, "people") are the members of the **congregation**, as distinguished from the clergy. Also used: *layman, laywoman, layperson.*

altar guild. A group in a church that cares for the altar, the sanctuary, and the preparations for Holy Communion. This includes tending to the altar linens, the altar vessels, the candles, the flowers, and the vestments. Sometimes called *altar society.*

catechumen. One who is receiving instruction in the **catechism**, with the intention of **baptism**, **confirmation**, or membership in the church.

deaconess. A woman consecrated to the work of the Lord, who assists in particular church ministries.

elder. Throughout the Bible, the elders were older men in the community who were given authority based on their age and experience. In the early Church, elders were spiritual overseers, and the term was used interchangeably with "**bishop**" (Acts 20:17, 28; Titus 1:5, 7). Standards for becoming an elder were stringent (1 Tim. 3:1–7; Titus 1:6–9), and their responsibilities included spiritual oversight and teaching (1 Tim. 5:17). Today, elders form the basis of church governance in the Presbyterian Church, where all the leaders in the church are elders or presbyters (Greek, *presbyterion,* "elder"), the pastor being the "teaching" elder. In other Protestant denominations, elders are responsible for the spiritual affairs of the church, while the deacons oversee the temporal affairs.

parishioner. A member of a parish.

trustee. A layperson elected to serve in a local church, particularly in matters of administration and finance.

usher. A person whose duty is to find seats for the worshipers and to receive their offering at the proper place in the service.

vestry. A group of lay people who, with the presiding cleric, are charged with the temporal affairs of a church. May be called a *council* or a *consistory* in some churches.

warden. A ranking lay officer of an Anglican (Episcopal) parish. Each parish vestry has two wardens (a senior warden and a junior warden) who manage the vestry and supervise their responsibilities.

SYMBOLS OF THE CHURCH

Ark, Noah's. A popular symbol in the early Church, mentioned by Peter as symbolic of **baptism** (1 Pet. 3:20–21), and later used by St. Gregory the Great as a symbol of the Church.

beehive. A more contemporary symbol of the Church, in which many work for the good of all.

dolphin. An ancient symbol, from Greek and Roman symbolism and adopted by the early Church because it did not arouse the suspicion of the authorities. In mythology, the dolphin carried souls to the island of the dead. In the early Church it retained its responsibility, representing the Church guiding souls into heaven. Associated also with the story of **Jonah**, where it represents salvation.

dove. A symbol used in the early Church speaking of the peace found in the community of faith, especially in times of great conflict. Often shown with an **olive branch**, particularly in scenes depicting stories of God's protection in time of danger.

fish. A follower of Jesus Christ, a member of his Church (Matt. 13:47–50). The fish is also often seen in symbols associated with **baptism** and the **Eucharist**, both sacraments of membership.

leaven (yeast). Represents the kingdom of heaven, especially the influence of Christianity (Matt. 13:33). This image was also used by Jesus to describe the pervasive (and evil) influence of the religious leaders (Matt. 16:6–12).

 **Orans.** (Latin, "praying.") A figure standing in an attitude of prayer, with arms raised at his or her sides, elbows bent, and palms facing forward. Borrowed from Greek and Roman imagery, this image is among the most common symbols used by the early Church; it appears in the catacombs and in other Christian art, often in representations of a variety of biblical stories. The Virgin Mary is often depicted in this posture of prayer, and a priest will assume this posture during the sacrament of Eucharist.

Often thought to represent the prayers of the deceased for the living, because of its use in the catacombs. May also symbolize the Church and its faith.

rock or **mountain** with a church standing on top: the Church founded on the rock, Jesus Christ (Matt. 7:24–27).

pillar. An early symbol of the Church, based on Paul's words to Timothy, describing the church as "the pillar and foundation of the truth" (1 Tim. 3:15).

pomegranate. This fruit with its many seeds represents the single Church composed of many members.

sheep, lambs. A follower of Jesus Christ, a member of his Church (John 10:1–8).

sheep (flock). The Church as the sheep of the **Good Shepherd**.

ship. A very early symbol of the Church, appearing in the catacombs. Like **Noah's Ark**, the ship carries souls safely through danger. Often shown sailing in restless waters. May feature a cross-shaped mast and one or more apostles. Recalls the occasion when Jesus and his disciples were in a boat on the Sea of Galilee, and Jesus calmed the storm (Matt. 8:23–27). See **nave**.

vine. An early symbol of the Church, derived from the Jewish tradition in which the vine represented the community of faith, specifically Israel and Judah (Isa. 5:1–7) and in the New Testament, believers abiding in Jesus Christ (John 15:1–11). Often shown with a dove, though grapes may also appear.

wheat and tares (or *weeds*). Believers and unbelievers; hence, the Church on earth (Matt. 13:24–30, 36–43).

TWELVE

Vestments

PRAYERS FOR VESTING

While washing the hands:
Give strength to my hands, Lord, to wipe away all stain,
so that I may be able to serve thee in purity of mind and body.

While placing the amice over the head:
Lord, set the helmet of salvation on my head
to fend off all the assaults of the devil.

While donning the alb:
Purify me, Lord, and cleanse my heart so that, washed in the
Blood of the Lamb,
I may enjoy eternal bliss.

While tying the cincture:
Lord, gird me with the cincture of purity and
extinguish my fleshly desires,
that the virtue of continence and chastity may abide within me.

While placing the maniple over the left arm
(Tridentine rite only):
Lord, may I worthily bear the maniple of tears and sorrow
so as to receive the reward of my labor with rejoicing.

While placing the stole around the neck:
Lord, restore the stole of immortality, which I lost through

the collusion of our first parents, and,
unworthy as I am to approach thy sacred mysteries, may I yet
gain eternal joy.

The deacon may use this prayer while donning the dalmatic:
Lord, endow me with the garment of salvation, the vestment of
joy, and may the dalmatic of justice ever encompass me.[75]

Vestments are the distinctive dress worn by the clergy, **choir, acolyte, crucifer, verger,** and others when performing the liturgical duties and participating in other ceremonies of the Church. Vestments, like many of the practices and traditions of the Church, are rooted in ancient practices—in this case the ceremonial garb of the ancient world. In the early Church, vestments were not particularly distinct from clothes worn by the general public. Eventually long tunics and mantles were discontinued in general wear, but the Christian clergy continued to use them in the church, as they had become associated with the ceremony and celebration of the liturgy. Gradually, a grand system of vestments evolved that to the modern worshiper is at once celebratory and mysterious—oddly appropriate to celebrating the sacramental mysteries!

Most vestments have functional, not simply ceremonial roots, based on practical concerns of staying warm and dry. Churches were unheated, and often priests did not even have the luxury of a roof over their heads! So capes and gloves and layers of clothing, no matter how distinctive and beautiful, served the higher purpose of protection against the elements.

The Reformation made its mark on vestments as well as on liturgical practice. Different churches had different policies and attitudes about vestments, but in general, the Reformers tended to simplify or in some cases eliminate vestments completely. Today Anglican and Protestant churches use vestments to varying degrees, but the standard remains with the Roman Church.

221

The vestments vary according to the hierarchical rank of the wearer and the function. Consider the importance of vestments to the worshiper who cannot read and has no way of determining who is who, and who is doing what when, except by the clothing.

There are three basic classifications of vestments for the priest:

- **liturgical dress** is used during the Mass and other liturgical functions by all clerics actively participating;
- **choir dress** is the most formal dress for clerics at liturgical events, worn by those attending but not participating at a liturgical event;
- **academic dress** is the vesture appropriate for the most formal nonliturgical events.

Vestments described here are those that may be seen in parish or diocesan worship services.

LITURGICAL DRESS[76]

ALL CLERGY

Alb, Amice, Biretta, Cassock, Cope, Stole

Bishop:	Priest:	Deacon:
Chasuble	Chasuble	Dalmatic
Dalmatic		
Gauntlets		
Zucchetto		
Pectoral Cross		
Miter		
Episcopal Ring		
Crosier		

VESTMENTS
Eucharistic And Other Vestments.

MITER   BIRETTA   MANIPLE   STOLE   COLLAR AND RABAT   CINCTURE   COTTA   DALMATIC

CASSOCK   AMICE OVER CASSOCK   ALB AND CINCTURE   STOLE AND MANIPLE

CHASUBLE   SURPLICE   CHIMERE   COPE

ALL CLERGY

alb. (Latin, *alba,* "white.") An ankle-length white vestment with sleeves symbolizing purity. It is worn by all clerics at liturgical celebrations. Tied at the waist with a **cincture**, it may be worn with a **stole** and **chasuble** over it.

amice. (Latin, *amicire,* "to cover.") A square or rectangular piece of white linen with two ties at the upper corners, worn over the shoulders with the **alb** to completely cover the neck and collar. Originally this vestment was intended to protect the Roman collar.

biretta. A square hat with three ridges and a tuft in the center. The one worn by the **regular clergy** is black, by the **bishop**, purple. (This vestment is now optional.) The holder of a doctorate degree may wear a biretta with four ridges.

cassock. The central vestment worn by the clergy, **acolytes**, **choristers**, and **organist**. Unchanged since the twelfth century, the cassock is floor-length, featuring a Roman collar and thirty-three buttons (representing the years of Christ's life on earth). It also has narrow sleeves, with a bodice that fits tight to the waist and a full skirt. Generally the cassock is black with black piping, although the color of the piping, buttons, or cassock itself can vary for **prelates**.

cincture. (Latin, "girdle.") Symbolic of priestly purity, a cincture is a rope with a tassel or a four-inch-wide band of silk with a fringe, worn around the waist over the **cassock** or **alb**. With the new fitted-style albs, the cincture may be an unnecessary vestment today.

cope. A flowing, full-length cape. It matches the color of the liturgy and is worn over an **alb** and **stole** at ceremonies other than the

Mass. It is fastened over the chest by a *morse*, a clasp made out of precious metals and sometimes ornamented with a precious jewel.

maniple. A long narrow strip of silk in **liturgical colors** worn as an ornament on the left forearm of the celebrant at **Mass**. Seldom used now except in Latin Masses.

stole. A long scarf of fabric matching the color of the liturgy and usually decorated with embroidered symbols. It is worn over the left shoulder and tied on the right side by **deacons** and over both shoulders by **priests** and **bishops** as a symbol of ordination, representing the yoke of Christ.

BISHOP

Vestments worn by bishops and other members of the higher clergy are sometimes called *episcopal vestments*.

bishop's ring. A signet ring bearing the seal of the diocese carved in an amethyst.

crosier, also **crozier.** (French, "cross-bearer.") A pastoral staff of wood or precious metal, shaped like a shepherd's crook, carried by **bishops** and **abbots** as a sign of the bishop's pastoral role and the ecclesiastical authority they exercise over their flock.

gauntlets. Liturgical gloves that may be used by bishops during liturgical celebrations (as celebrant or concelebrant, not in choir). Made of silk, they may match the liturgical color or may be white, and extend partially past the wrist. Wearing these gloves became optional after Vatican II.

miter. The headdress worn by archbishops, bishops, and abbots at liturgical functions as a symbol of authority. It has two fringed lappets hanging down at the back. The pope wears a triple miter, sometimes called a *tiara*.

pectoral cross. (Latin, *pectoralis*, "breast.") A small cross, usually about six inches in height, worn on a chain around the neck and resting on the chest over the heart. Originally worn only by **bishops**, the pectoral cross is now commonly used by the **regular clergy**.

zucchetto. The silk skullcap worn by Roman Catholic **bishops**. The color of the skullcap varies according to the rank of the wearer.

PRIEST

chasuble. (Latin, "little house.") A vestment made of silk or other material, matching the color of the liturgy. The celebrant wears it over the **alb** and **stole** at **Holy Communion** and high festivals. It is oval-shaped and sleeveless, with an opening for the head near the center. The celebrant may don this vestment immediately before beginning the Holy Communion or may wear it throughout the **Mass**.

humeral veil. The oblong shawl-like vestment worn around the shoulders and over the hands by a priest who is carrying the **ciborium** as it is moved from one place to another.

DEACON

dalmatic. A silk tuniclike vestment worn by ordained assistants (**deacons**) to the celebrant at the celebration of **Holy Communion** and by the **bishop** under the **chasuble** at observances of major solemnity. This vestment can vary in design, with open or closed sides, ample or cut sleeves, ankle or knee-length. A similar vestment worn by the **subdeacon** is called a *tunic* (or *tunicle*).

CHOIR DRESS[77]

Bishop:	Monsignor:	Priest and under:
Biretta	Biretta	Biretta
Cassock	Cassock	Cassock
Rochet	Surplice	Surplice
Fascia	*Fascia*	
Zucchetto		
Mozzetta		
Cappa Magna		
Episcopal Ring		
Pectoral Cross		

CHOIR DRESS FOR A BISHOP OR METROPOLITAN

cappa magna. The full-length outer garment with a train and attached shoulder cape worn on very solemn occasions. Rarely used since Vatican II.

fascia. The familiar silk sash with fringe used originally as a **cincture** by **bishops** and other **prelates**. Its color varies according to the rank of the wearer.

mantelletta. Knee-length sleeveless vestment of silk or wool covering the **rochet**, worn by cardinals, **bishops**, and other **prelates**.

mozzetta. The short shoulder cape with a small ornamental hood, worn over the **cassock** and **rochet** by **bishops** and other **prelates**. It is made of the same material and color as the cassock.

pallium. A white woolen band with pendants in front and back worn over the **chasuble** by archbishops, patriarchs, and the pope as a symbol of full episcopal authority. It is a thin band of white wool that circles the neck, with extensions front and back. It is generally richly embroidered and marked with several black crosses.

rochet. A knee-length white linen vestment worn over the **cassock** by **bishops**. It is somewhat like the **surplice**, but has close-fitting sleeves and often may be a fancy garment, made out of lace and linen.

CHOIR DRESS FOR A PRIEST AND DEACON

surplice. A very common white vestment worn by a minister over a cassock. It extends in length at least to the minister's knees and falls full and freely about his person. The seasonal **stole** is placed over the surplice.

DISTINCT TO ANGLICAN CLERGY

chimere. A loose sleeveless robe worn by some Anglican bishops over the **rochet**.

tippet. A broad black scarf worn over the **surplice** by the Anglican clergy during Morning and Evening Prayer.

VESTMENT ORNAMENTATION

galloon. A narrow trimming (lace, embroidery, or braid with both edges scalloped) woven in ecclesiastical design and applied as an edging on a **dossal**, **paraments**, and vestments.

orphrey. An ornate band of embroidery used to decorate ecclesiastical vestments, such as the **cope**, **chasuble**, etc.

GENERAL VESTMENTS

clerical collar. A stiff linen or plastic collar, either single or double, fastening in the back and worn with a **rabat**.

cotta. (Latin, "coat.") A white vestment with large sleeves and yoke, with fullness extending to the fingertips. As a symbol of purity, it is worn over the **cassock** by the **acolyte**, **chorister**, and **organist**. It is the counterpart of the **surplice** of the clergy.

Geneva gown. A black academic gown worn by the minister in less liturgical churches.

rabat. A vestlike garment covering the chest. Made on a neckband, it is worn with a clerical collar by the clergy. Black is the preferred color.

VESTMENTS OF MONASTIC ORDERS

cowl or **hood.** Usually the long, hooded cloak worn by monks, but also may refer to an unattached hood worn by some orders.

girdle. Like the **cincture**, the girdle serves as a symbol of purity (chastity) and spiritual readiness.

habit. The distinctive dress of those committed to God's work, especially the clergy and those in holy orders. The usual colors are black, white, gray, brown, or blue. May also be called *garb*. Consists of a **tunic**, belt or girdle, **scapular**, hood for men and **veil** for women, and a **mantle** for use in choir and out of doors.

mantle. A vestment regarded as a symbol of preeminence or authority.

 **scapular.** A band of cloth worn front and back over the shoulders as part of a monastic **habit**. It measures between fourteen and eighteen inches wide, reaches almost to the feet, and has an opening for the head.

tonsure. The shaved crown or patch worn by monks and other clerics.

tunic. The unadorned basic garment of a monastic **habit**.

veil. The outer covering of a **nun's** headdress, often worn over a wimple.

wimple. The cloth covering worn over the head and around the neck and chin by women in the late medieval period and as part of the **habit** for some orders of **nuns**.

Notes

INTRODUCTION TO THE FIRST EDITION

1. Thomas C. Oden, *Ministry through Word and Sacrament* (Grand Rapids, MI: Baker Books, 1994), 77–78.

ONE
SACRED PLACES, SACRED SPACES

2. Romano Guardini, *Sacred Signs* (St. Louis: Pio Decimo Press, 1956), 37–38.

3. Ibid., 39.

4. Ibid., 40.

TWO
THE ALTAR

5. Guardini, *Sacred Signs*, 74–75.

6. Hannah Ward and Jennifer Wild, comps., *The Doubleday Christian Quotation Collection* (New York: Doubleday, 1998), entry 7:19, 47.

7. Guardini, *Sacred Signs*, 70–71.

8. Ibid., 57–58.

9. *The Divine Liturgy according to the Maronite Antiochian Rite* (Detroit: Maronite Chancery Office, 1969).

THREE
THE CROSS

10. Alexander Bogolepov, *Orthodox Hymns* (Crestwood, NY: St. Vladimir's Press, 1976), LTP Triduum 4.

11. *Byzantine Daily Worship* (Allendale, NJ: Alleluia Press, 1969).

FOUR
THE LITURGICAL YEAR

12. Thomas Merton, "Time and the Liturgy" (1955), *Seasons of Celebration* (New York: Farrar, Straus and Giroux, 1965), 48–49.

13. Ibid., 49.

14. J.A. Jungman, *Pastoral Liturgy* (New York: Herder and Herder, 1962).

15. John Shea, trans., from the foreword to *The Eternal Year* by Karl Rahner (Baltimore: Helicon Press, Inc., 1964), 9–10.

16. Thomas Merton, "The Nativity Kerygma" (1956), *Seasons of Celebration*, 102.

17. Peter Chrysologus, in the "Office of Readings" from *The Liturgy of the Hours*, V. I. (New York: The Catholic Book Company, 1975), 557–58.

18. Pius Parsch, *Sermons on the Liturgy for Sundays and Feast Days*, trans. Phillip T. Weller (Milwaukee, WI: The Bruce Publishing Company, 1953).

19. Guardini, *Sacred Signs*, 54.

20. Theodulph, *A Lent Sourcebook: The Forty Days*, Book Two (Chicago: Liturgical Training Publications, 1990), 175.

21. Karl Rahner, *The Eternal Year* (Baltimore: Helicon Press, Inc., 1964), 87–88.

22. From *The Book of Common Prayer 1979* of the Episcopal Church, USA, 355.

23. Bert Ghezzi, *Voices of the Saints: A Year Book of Readings* (New York: Doubleday, 2000), 608.

24. A. Hamman, ed., Walter Mitchell, trans., *Early Christian Prayers* (Chicago: Henry Regnery Company, 1961), 76.

FIVE
LITURGICAL WORSHIP

25. Evelyn Underhill, *Worship* (Guildford, England: Eagle, an imprint of Inter Publishing Service Ltd., 1991), 63–64.

26. Excerpt from the English translation of a reading in the *Liturgy of the Hours* (Washington, D.C.: International Committee of English in the Liturgy, Inc., 1974).

27. From *The Book of Common Prayer* 1979.

28. Guardini, *Sacred Signs*, 59.

29. In the Anglican rite, the portions of the service shown in brackets are not generally part of today's services.

30. A. Hamman, ed., Walter Mitchell, trans., *Early Christian Prayers* (Chicago: Henry Regnery Company, 1961), 117–18.

31. Patrick O'Connor, ed., Alfonso M. diNola, comp., *The Prayers of Man: From Primitive Peoples to Present Times* (New York: I. Obolensky, 1961).

32. From *The Book of Common Prayer* 1979, 355.

33. Ibid., 351.

34. Balthasar Fischer, *Signs, Words, and Gestures,* trans. Michael J. O'Connell (New York: Pueblo Publishing Company, 1981), 33.

35. From *The Book of Common Prayer* 1979, 324.

36. From *The Book of Common Prayer* 1979, 356.

37. Fischer, *Signs, Words, and Gestures,* 34.

38. James McKinnon, ed., *Music in Early Christian Literature* (New York: Cambridge University Press, 1987).

39. F. L. Cross, ed., *St. Cyril of Jerusalem's Lectures on the Christian Sacraments* (Crestwood, NY: St. Vladimir Press, 1986).

40. "Mediator Dei," as quoted in Gabe Huck, ed., *A Sourcebook about Liturgy* (Chicago: Liturgical Training Publications, 1994), 177.

SIX
THE MUSIC OF WORSHIP

41. Alan J. Hommerding and Diana Kodner, comps., *A Sourcebook about Music* (Chicago: Liturgy Training Publications, 1997), 101.

42. A. Hamman, ed., Walter Mitchell, trans., *Early Christian Prayers* (Chicago: Henry Regnery Company, 1961), 29.

43. From *The Book of Common Prayer* 1979, 92.

44. Ibid., 91–92.

45. Ibid., 93.

46. Ibid., 95.

47. Ibid., 82.

48. Hildegard of Bingen, *Hildegard von Bingen's Mystical Visions,* translated from *Scivias* by Bruce Hozeski (Santa Fe, NM: Bear & Company, 1995).

49. *The Geneva Psalter* by John Calvin, 1543.

50. Thomas C. Oden, *Ministry through Word and Sacrament* (New York: Crossroad Publishing Company, 1989).

SEVEN
THE SACRAMENTS

51. Henri Nouwen, *Bread for the Journey* (San Francisco: HarperSanFrancisco, 1997), entry for September 22.

52. E. Theodore Bachmann, ed., *Luther's Works*, Vol. 35 in *Word and Sacrament* (Philadelphia: Concordia Publishing House and Muhlenberg Press, 1960).

53. Gabe Huck, ed., *A Sourcebook about Liturgy* (Chicago: Liturgical Training Press, 1994), 135.

54. From *The Book of Common Prayer* 1979, 419.

55. Ibid., 456.

56. Michael Counsell, comp., *2000 Years of Prayer* (Harrisburg, PA: Morehouse, 1999), 490.

57. Nathan Mitchell, *Background and Directions*, vol. 3 in *The Rite of Penance: Commentaries* (Silver Spring, MD: The Liturgical Conference, 1975).

EIGHT
PRIVATE WORSHIP

58. Dallas Willard, *The Spirit of the Disciplines: Understanding How God Changes Lives* (New York: HarperCollins Publishers, 1988), ix.

59. Fischer, *Signs, Words, and Gestures,* 50

60. Norvene Vest, *Bible Reading for Spiritual Growth* (San Francisco: HarperSanFrancisco, 1993), ix.

61. Richard Foster, *Prayer: Finding the Heart's True Home* (San Francisco: HarperSanFrancisco, 1992), 13.

62. C. S. Lewis, *An Experiment in Criticism* (Cambridge, England: Cambridge University Press, 1961), 17–18.

63. C. S. Lewis, *Letters to Malcolm: Chiefly on Prayer* (New York: Harcourt, Brace, Jovanovich, 1963, 1964), 17.

64. Guardini, *Sacred Signs,* 20.

65. Ibid., 22.

66. Ibid., 18.

67. Ibid., 30.

68. Brennen Manning, *Abba's Child* (Colorado Springs, CO: NavPress/Piñon Press, 1994), 55.

NINE
LESSONS AND BOOKS OF WORSHIP

69. Counsell, *2000 Years of Prayer*, 195.

TEN
WE BELIEVE

70. Dorothy L. Sayers, *Creed or Chaos* (Manchester, NH: Sophia Institute Press, 1995. Originally published by Harcourt, Brace, Inc., 1949), 31–32.

71. From *The Book of Common Prayer* 1979, 96.

72. English Language Liturgical Consultation translation, 1988.

73. From *The Book of Common Prayer* 1979, 864–65.

ELEVEN
THE BODY OF CHRIST

74. Romano Guardini, *The Church and the Catholic,* trans. Ada Lane (New York: Sheed & Ward, Inc., 1953).

TWELVE
VESTMENTS

75. Ian Rutherford (webmaster), "The Catholic Liturgical Library," www.catholicliturgy.com, © 1998–1999.

76. Joseph Shetler (jshetler@ghg.net), from his former Web page, "Roman Catholic Vestments." Used by permission.

77. Ibid.

Sources

Apostolos-Cappadona, Diane. *Dictionary of Christian Art*. New York: The Continuum Publishing Company, 1994.

Appleton, LeRoy H., and Stephen Bridges. *Symbolism in Liturgical Art*. New York: Charles Scribner's Sons, 1959.

Baldock, John. *The Elements of Christian Symbolism*. Tisbury, England: Element, 1997.

Bradner, John. *Symbols of the Church Seasons & Days*. Wilton, CT: Morehouse-Barlow Company, 1977.

Catholic Church. *Catechism of the Catholic Church. Catechismus Ecclesiae Catholicae. English*. Vatican City: Libreria Editrice Vaticana; Mahwah, NJ: [distributed by] Paulist Press, 1994.

Cross, F. L., editor. *The Oxford Dictionary of the Christian Church*. New York: Oxford University Press, 1957.

Eckel, Frederick L., Jr. *A Concise Dictionary of Ecclesiastical Terms*. Nashville: Abingdon Press, 1960.

Ferguson, George Wells. *Signs & Symbols in Christian Art*. New York: Oxford University Press, 1989.

Freedman, David Noel, editor-in-chief. *The Anchor Bible Dictionary* (6 volumes). New York: Doubleday, a division of Random House, Inc., 1992.

Gent, Barbara, and Betty Sturges. *The New Altar Guild Book*. Harrisburg, PA: Morehouse Publishing Company, 1996.

Griffith, Helen Stuart. *The Sign Language of Our Faith*. New York: Morehouse-Gorham Co., 1945.

Guardini, Romano. *Sacred Signs*. Grace Branham, translator. St. Louis: Pio Decimo Press, 1956.

Hatchett, Marion J. *Commentary on the American Prayer Book*. New York: Seabury Press, 1980.

Heller, Christopher. *The New Complete Server*. Harrisburg, PA: Morehouse Publishing Company, 1995.

237

Hynes, Mary Ellen. *Companion to the Calendar.* Chicago: Liturgy Training Publications, 1993.

Johnson, Kevin Orlin. *Why Do Catholics Do That?* New York: Ballantine Books, 1994.

McBrien, Richard P., general editor. *The HarperCollins Encyclopedia of Catholicism.* New York: HarperCollins, 1995.

Moe, Dean L. *Christian Symbols Handbook: Commentary and Patterns for Traditional and Contemporary Symbols.* Minneapolis: Augsburg Fortress Publications, 1990.

Moore, Stephen E. *Church Words: Origins and Meanings.* Cincinnati: Forward Movement Publications, 1996.

Murray, Peter, and Linda Murray. *The Oxford Companion to Christian Art and Architecture.* New York: Oxford University Press, 1998.

Post, Willard Ellwood. *Saints, Signs and Symbols.* Harrisburg, PA: Morehouse Publishing Company, 1962, 1974.

Price, Charles G., and Louis Weil. *Liturgy for Living.* San Francisco: HarperSanFrancisco, 1979.

Rest, Friedrich O. *Our Christian Symbols.* Illustrated by Harold Minton. Cleveland, OH: Pilgrim Press, 1975.

Shepherd, Massey Hamilton, Jr. *The Oxford American Prayer Book Commentary.* New York: Oxford University Press, 1950.

Strasser, Bernard. *With Christ Through the Year.* Milwaukee, WI: The Bruce Publishing Company, 1947.

Taylor, B. Don. *The Complete Training Course for Altar Guilds.* Harrisburg, PA: Morehouse Publishing Company, 1993.

Van Treeck, Carl, and Aloysius Croft, M.A. *Symbols in the Church.* Milwaukee, WI: The Bruce Publishing Company, 1936.

Vitz, Evelyn Birge. *A Continual Feast.* New York: Harper & Row Publishers, Inc., 1985.

Walsh, Michael. *Dictionary of Catholic Devotions.* San Francisco: HarperSanFrancisco, 1993.

Webber, F. R. *Church Symbolism*. Cleveland, OH: J. H. Jansen, Publishers, 1938.

Wetzler, Robert, and Helen Huntington. *Seasons and Symbols: a Handbook on the Church Year.* Minneapolis: Augsburg Publishing House, 1962.

Whittemore, Carroll E., editor. *Symbols of the Church*. Nashville: Abingdon Press, 1959.

Whone, Herbert. *Church Monastery Cathedral*. Tisbury, England: Element, 1990.

Wilde, James A., editor. *At That Time*. Chicago: Liturgy Training Publications, 1989.

Internet sites:
Ian Rutherford (webmaster), "The Catholic Liturgical Library," www.catholicliturgy.com, copyright © 1998–1999.

Bible translations
http://www.bible-researcher.com/versions.html
Contents copyright © 2001–2006 by Michael D. Marlowe.

Index

sun, moon, and eleven
stars, bowing to Joseph
[see Joseph]
sun, moon, and twelve
stars [see Jacob]
Sunday, 42
superfrontals [see
frontlets]
surplice, 228
Sursum Corda [see
Dialogue]
swastica [see Crux
Gammata]
sword, 72, 77
sword and trumpet [see
Joshua]
sword, broken and lance
(spear) [see Micah]
sword lily [see iris]
symbol [see creed]
symbols of John the
Baptist [see St. John
the Baptist, Nativity of]
symbols of saints, 73

T
tabernacle, 32
table for the bread of the
Presence [see Furniture
of the Tabernacle and
Temple]
tables, 178
Tablets of Stone [see
Ten Commandments]
tambourine [see
Miriam]
Tanakh [see Bible]
tau (form of cross), 39
Te Deum, 144
temple on a mountain
[see Micah]
Temple, model of [see
Solomon]
Temple, plan of the New
[see Ezekiel]
Temple, under construc-
tion [see Solomon, also
Haggai]

Temporal Cycle, 44, 48
Temporale [see
Temporal Cycle]
Ten Commandments,
129, 177
ten plagues [see Exodus]
tenebrae, 60
Terce, 119
tester, 23
tetramorph [see
Ezekiel]
thanksgiving, 124
Theos [see *Eloah*]
Theotokos [see Mary]
**Thirty-Nine Articles of
Religion,** 186
thistles [see brambles]
three fishes, 197
Three Hours, the, 60
thorns [see brambles]
throne, 22
thurible [see censer]
thurifer, 127, 216
tiara [see miter]
timbers [see Haggai]
tippet, 228
tithe, 134
tonsure, 230
torch, 62
torches [see candles]
tower, 77
Tower of Babel, 102
Tower of David, 81
Tower of ivory, 82
tracery, 10
tract, 122
tract [see also alleluia]
transept, 15
Transfiguration, the, 93
transubstantiation, 156
tree of life [see Adam
and Eve]
tree of the knowledge of
good and evil [see
Adam and Eve]
trefoil, 197
triangle, 198
Tribulation, 205

Triduum [see Paschal
Triduum]
Trinity (form of cross),
39
Trinity Season [see
Ordinary Time 2]
Trinity Sunday, 67
triple tiara, 77
triptych [see altarpiece]
triquetra, 197, 198
Trisagion, 129
triumph, cross of [see
triumphant]
Triumph of the Cross
[see Holy Cross Day]
**triumphant (form of
cross),** 39
trumpet [see Hosea,
Joel]
**trumpet, held by an
angel,** 205
trustee, 216
tunic, 230
tunic, tunicle [see
dalmatic]
Turris davidica [see
Tower of David]
Turris eburnea [see
Tower of ivory]
Twelfth day [see
Epiphany]
Twelfth night [see
Twelve days of
Christmas]
**Twelve Days of
Christmas,** 51
two altars [see Cain and
Abel]
two caves [see Obadiah]
two columns out of
plumb [see Samson]
two tables of stone [see
Exodus]

U
unction [see Anointing
of the Sick]
unleavened bread, 155